Those
PREACHING
Women

A Multicultural
Collection

Those
PREACHING
Women

A Multicultural
Collection

Edited by Ella Pearson Mitchell
and Valerie Bridgeman Davis

Foreword by Katie G. Cannon

JUDSON PRESS
PUBLISHERS SINCE 1824
VALLEY FORGE, PA

The editors and Judson Press have made every effort to trace the ownership of all
quotes. In the event of a question arising from the use of a quote, we regret any error
made and will be pleased to make the necessary correction in future printings and edi-
tions of this book.

Bible quotations in this volume are from Good News Translation (GNB)—Second Edition Copyright © 1992 by American Bible Society. Used by permission; *The Holy Bible*,
King James Version (KJV); The New King James Version (NKJV). Copyright © 1972,
1984 by Thomas Nelson Inc.; the HOLY BIBLE, NEW INTERNATIONAL VER-
SION®. NIV®. (NIV). Copyright© 1973, 1978, 1984 by International Bible Society. Used
by permission of Zondervan. All rights reserved.; the New Revised Standard Version of
the Bible (NRSV), copyright © 1989 by the Division of Christian Education of the
National Council of the Churches of Christ in the U.S.A. Used by permission; the
Revised Standard Version of the Bible (RSV), copyright © 1946, 1952, 1971 by the Division of Christian Education of the National Council of the Churches of Christ in the
U.S.A. Used by permission.

Library of Congress Cataloging-in-Publication Data

Those preaching women : a multicultural collection / Ella Pearson Mitchell and Valerie
Bridgeman Davis, editors ; foreword by Katie G. Cannon. — 1st ed.
 p. cm.
 ISBN 978-0-8170-1537-4 (pbk. : alk. paper) 1. Sermons, American—Women
authors. 2. Women clergy—United States. I. Mitchell, Ella Pearson. II. Davis, Valerie
Bridgeman.
 BV4241.T476 2008
 252—dc22

2008007947

Printed on recycled paper in the U.S.A.
First Edition, 2008.

*To the cloud of witnesses of those
preachin' women who have gone before us
and to those yet to come*

Contents

Old Testament Sermons

New Testament Sermons

Foreword

I imagine that the Rev. Dr. Ella P. Mitchell is once again sending forth a prayer of thanksgiving upon receiving her copy of *Those Preaching Women: A Multicultural Collection,* the most recent volume of prophetic sermons brought to fruition. Since graduating from Union Theological Seminary (New York City) in 1943, Dr. Mitchell has made a point of mentoring churchwomen. Over the span of her ministerial vocation, single-handedly Dr. Mitchell has supported and encouraged the preaching gifts of African American clergywomen, an effort that resulted in the publication of the original four installments of *Those Preaching Women* (1985, 1994, 1996, and 2004), sermon anthologies that expanded steadily over the past twenty-three years. She is heralded across this nation as the dean of black women preachers.

However, this latest volume of *Those Preaching Women* is a venture into new territory. Racial diversity is the essence of this anthology. As the latest book in this series, *Those Preaching Women: A Multicultural Collection* is a treasure trove that includes the unfettered, creative exchange of sacred rhetoric by women from Vietnam, Cuba, and the Shinnecock Nation. The moment of epiphany that led to this tangible collection of sermons edited by the Rev. Dr. Valerie Bridgeman Davis occurred during the Festival of Women of Color Preachers, April 30 to May 4, 2007, at the National Cathedral College of Preachers in Washington, D.C. It was during this event that Mitchell and Bridgeman Davis extended an invitation to Native American, Asian American, Latina American, and African American women to share their homiletical gifts. Bridgeman Davis reached out, tracked down, and gathered sermons from women of color that never would have come together otherwise.

The vitality of these sermons comes from their power on two levels: that of excellent exegesis of biblical texts—stories such as Hagar and Ishmael in the desert of Beersheba, Samuel anointing David as the future king, Amnon's crime of rape against his sister Tamar, the healing of Naaman the leper, Queen Vashti refusing to parade before King Ahasuerus, the annunciation of the births of John and Jesus, the desire to build tabernacles on the Mount of Transfiguration, the passion of Christ, the day of Pentecost—and that of proclaiming life lessons from canonized Scripture that connect to our lived context. This synergy between the Bible and embodiment, between "thus saith the Lord" and "here I am, Lord," brings to light stunning parallels between the biblical world and our contemporary society, deepening our understanding of authentic Christian discipleship.

From sermons such as Donna Allen's presentation of Jeremiah the weeping prophet in "A Cracked Cistern, a Living God" to Sakena D. Young-Scaggs's maneuvers through the storms of life in "Spiritual Alchemy," the writers of this sacred rhetoric communicate a generous offering of unforgettable images imprinted from our childhood, churchgoing memories, and invaluable testimonies about God's promises of restoration and protection. We, their readers, receive in turn invitations to explore images of living water that flow out of the believer's heart and to assess the difference between sowing sparingly and reaping bountifully. Intrinsically intertwined are sound warnings about warring congregations and hopeful visions of the possibilities for unity in the body of Christ. The sermons in this volume bring vividly to life the crucifixion of Jesus, the imprisonment of Paul and Silas, and stories of persecution that occur when we obey God rather than humans. Despite their often weighty matters of theology and ethics, these sermons are also heartwarming and joyful, full of anecdotes that are laugh-out-loud funny.

These thirty-three women preachers offer us sermons that expand our horizons and enliven our souls. They provide answers to many of the questions our youth are asking. For all the differences of race, class, ethnicity, denominational affiliation, ordination status, and theological ideas reflected in this volume, each sermon is intellectually, emotionally, and spiritually demanding. In bygone days, the theology of racial-ethnic churchwomen could scarcely be heard in pulpits. Today these preachers declare their divinely inspired messages in a distinctly indicative voice. Roaring with life, they share with us sparkling gems of usable wisdom that run the gamut—from living in the between time to extemporaneous proclamations that force us to rethink what we thought we understood about slavery, the Trail of Tears, neocolonialism, globalization, and HIV/AIDS. These sermons take us to the internal chamber of our sickest secrets and offer resources for holistic healing. What's more, this volume exhibits a dazzling array of experiences, preaching venues, and professional expertise—a clarion testimony that women have, indeed, been involved in every human endeavor.

—Katie G. Cannon, MDiv, MPhil, PhD
Annie Scales Rogers Professor of Christian Social Ethic
Union Theological Seminary
and Presbyterian School of Christian Education

Preface

Editing another person's words is a sacred trust, so I have counted this project as a call from God to handle carefully these words. As one who teaches preachers in my professional life, I am always interested in what moves the preacher. And no matter her ethnic background, each of these women cares about changing the world through justice making. The passion for women as widows, as victims of rape, as HIV/AIDS sufferers, and more, comes through the words of these sermons, which reflect that human needs and concerns cross social, class, ethnic, and racial divides.

I made two decisions in preparing this volume that may or may not be helpful to students of preaching or to those who care about these words. The first decision was to list the moments when these sermons were first, and sometimes severally, preached. As a quasi-historian, I always wonder about the context in which words were first spoken and what the preacher may have had in mind when she was preparing. I am fascinated to know whether a sermon was prepared for a particular context or only for this moment in which the congregation is conceived as the reading public. This decision seemed apparent to me in its value, but as it may reflect only my idiosyncrasies, I alone am responsible for it.

The value of the second decision—to add endnotes—may be less apparent. Again, the decision came from my role as a teacher. Notes allow readers to understand some of the conversational partners who informed a sermon. This decision was not intended to make the sermon an essay; instead, it is an attempt to uncover parts of the sermonic process often unheard by the hearer or unseen by the reader.

Since these sermons are not proclaimed from the pulpit but rather in the happy repose of the reader's armchair or the student's desk, it seemed essential to me that readers have at their disposal, as much as prudent, the ability to judge sources. (The necessity of editing the sermons in length means that some of the referenced conversational partners were also cut.)

Readers are asked to remember that orality has with it dramatic pauses and congregational responses, as well as body language to make the added emphases. And stories hold the imagination of the audience. It is no small feat to delete what in the moment of proclamation was no doubt a powerful word but in the reading does not hold. What the written text lacks that the spoken word rejoices in is the call and response of listeners who are desperate to hear a word from God. Many of the sermons arrived in preaching form, that is, the preachers left their notes for pauses, for extra stories, and for interaction with the audience in the margins. It was tempting to leave these as a gift to the reader, a rare treat to know what the preacher has emphasized in speech. However, in almost all of the sermons, I removed prefatory remarks and began where the actual engagement with the text or story began. That decision alone substantially cut many of the sermons. We removed the verbal calls for response (e.g., "Is anyone listening to me?" or "Do you see what I'm saying?" or "Look to your neighbor."). Some painful cuts had to be made, such as Lisa Davison's colorfully told story of her friendship with a lab rat that was eventually fed to the lab snake, or Gayll Phifer-Houseman's poignant recounting of the adoption of her four Ethiopian children. We also made a hard decision to remove all the italicized and bold words, which may have cued the reader to the preachers' concerns. Instead, we, the readers, are left to imagine the moment of proclamation and to add our own emphases. I can only hope that such editing has not done violence to the spirit of the preachers' texts. Still, I trust that the sermons offered in this volume will testify to the power of imagery, of passion, and of conviction.

In large part, pragmatic space constraints guided our decision to provide within these pages a truncated version of the sermons offered. We had to decide: do we provide as many voices of women preachers at the beginning of the twenty-first century as possible, or do we limit the number of voices in order to include longer sermons? In the end, it made sense to present the maximum number of sermons in a representative form. I say "representative" to indicate that something is missing, although for the sake of readability, I decided against using ellipses, which would have indicated to the reader where cuts and skips were made. Of course, I do have as a concern that someone will read a sermon and say, "Hey! I was there. This sermon is nothing like the one I heard." Editing is interpretation. I trust that I have left the preachers' own flavor in the body of the sermons, even when I have had to cut them substantially.

Even with editorial cuts, several themes have seeped through most all the sermons, no matter the theological starting point or the ethnic background of the writer. Among those themes are the notions of an inclusive, expansive, extravagant grace; table fellowship as the community-building location of the reign of God; diversity of persons and experience as a high value and vision for what humanity looks like at its best; and varying levels of commitment to all kinds of social justice, and not just social service.

Finally, I want to express my deep gratitude to the Rev. Dr. Ella P. Mitchell, dean of black women preachers. As she, Katie Cannon, and I sat in the refectory at the Washington Cathedral's College of Preachers one evening in May 2007, I was moved and encouraged by the tales she told of her history. Mother Mitchell's life is storied and profound. After about an hour of sharing horror and honor stories from our lives as ministers in the church, she said to me, "Valerie, you're so brave!" When I asked why she said it, she simply replied, "Because you are." At the time and even now, I received the words as a prophetic blessing into my life as a professor, a minister, and a scholar. I do not feel particularly brave. But words spoken to us, and through us, have power. I bravely and humbly offer these words to our readers as a gift from God through God's women from every tribe, nation, and language.

—Valerie Bridgeman Davis
Memphis, Tennessee

Acknowledgments

No volume or book comes to fruition without the constant and dedicated support of many people. We and all the contributors bring our histories into this project, so there are many more people than the ones named here who are owed our gratitude.

We especially want to thank the congregations and conferences that received these sermons in their various settings.

Special thanks to Catharine Cummings, Don Davis, and Dr. Henry H. Mitchell for their eye for detail, flow, and grammar as they helped us edit these pieces.

Thank you to Emilygail Dill for her generous and unflagging support of this project, and especially for her continued friendship and care of Ella Mitchell.

Thanks to those persons at the publishing house, especially Lisa Blair, who chased down details and pictures to get this project done in record time, and Rebecca Irwin-Diehl, who also believed another volume was timely and desirable.

To God be the glory!

Introduction

When I was writing my doctoral dissertation in 1973, I was also serving as president of educational ministries for the American Baptist Churches in the USA. I had an idea that my research might become a helpful resource for holistic growth in churches. An outline for a year-long curriculum based on Luke 2:52 was clear in my mind.

Judson Press, which is the publishing ministry of the ABCUSA, was not favorably disposed to my proposal—my position with the denomination notwithstanding—but they had a proposal of their own for me. "Why don't you invite a number of women preachers to submit sermons to a volume for publication?" they offered. It was not what I wanted to hear. It was, however, "the more excellent way," and for that, I am deeply grateful.

Those Preachin' Women (TPW) appeared in 1985 and offered a collection of sermons by African American women representing various church traditions and different ministry settings: from pastors (a precious few) to denominational executives. In those days, there were but a handful of ordained clergywomen.

By the time volumes 2 and 3 of *Those Preaching Women* were released in 1988 and 1996, respectively, there were more and more seminary-trained African American women, and a growing number of them were going on to pursue ordination and pastoral ministry.

Those Preaching Women, volume 4, was released in 2004, and it, too, was a collection of sermons by twenty-five black women of diverse denominations and ministry settings. My dear friend and student, Jackie Glass, was my able and enthusiastic coeditor. We were sure we had reached the limits of the series and were content to glean proceeds from the promotion of *TPW4* for several small scholarships to aid women in seminary.

Those Preaching Women: A Multicultural Collection appears now at the urging of women who, encouraged in their ministries by the previous contributors, wish to be included among those preaching women in whose paths they follow. Again, these women come from many church traditions and various ministry settings, and this time they represent many of the racial-ethnic origins America now claims.

My profound gratitude goes to Rev. Dr. Valerie Bridgeman Davis, who is my coeditor for the project. This volume sees the light of day due in large measure to her "persistent knock." To God be the glory!

—Ella Pearson Mitchell
Atlanta, Georgia

Old Testament
SERMONS

1

Awaken to God's Dreams

Daisy L. Machado

GENESIS 21:14-21

And God heard the voice of the boy; and the angel of God called to Hagar from heaven, and said to her, "What troubles you, Hagar? Do not be afraid; for God has heard the voice of the boy where he is." (Genesis 21:17, NRSV)

This story is all about Sarai and Hagar, but it is Hagar who calls out to my heart. The story comes to a tragic, bitter end in the relationship between two women who for years shared a roof and the protection of a common household. And for Hagar, the loss of community is not just about being left alone or about being left out. To lose her community or tribe was to endanger her ability to survive. To lose the safety of her tribe made her even more foreign, even more alien, even more unwanted.

Hagar wanders into and out of the lives of the first ancestors of Israel, and she brings with her great change. We first meet Hagar in Genesis 16:1-2, which declares, "Now Sarai, Abram's wife, bore him no children. She had an Egyptian slave-girl whose name was Hagar, and Sarai said to Abram, 'You see that the Lord has prevented me from bearing children; go in to my slave-girl; it may be that I shall obtain children by her.'" We do not know when Hagar may have joined Abram and Sarai, perhaps when they sojourned into Egypt in order to survive a famine. We may not know *when* she came into Abram's household, but we do know that because of her ethnic background, Hagar was different from Abram and Sarai: a different race

3

and a different religion. And her differences made her vulnerable and dependent upon them for her own survival.

That is precisely why Sarai uses her powerless maidservant to bring forth the heir she and Abram so desperately desire but cannot conceive. Sarai sees Hagar as her tool, a means to an end. Sarai uses Hagar's powerlessness to achieve the coveted heir, a common practice in her times. it seems that Sarai's impatience about God's promise led her to abuse Hagar's vulnerability.

But after the birth of Ishmael, it soon becomes clear to both women that they cannot live together any longer. And Hagar probably knew that once she became pregnant, her role within the household changed; her status was elevated and she now took rank over her mistress.[1] Sarai resents Hagar's superior attitude and, with Abram's approval, determines to put the younger woman back in her place. When Sarai mistreats Hagar (see Genesis 14:6), the pregnant Hagar runs away because she will not tolerate abuse. Mistreated by her mistress and ignored by Abram, who abdicates any responsibility, Hagar goes from slavery to homelessness. And she must face her suffering alone.[2]

That's when God intervenes. The angel of God finds Hagar in the desert at the well on the road to Shur. The angel's message to Hagar contains both heartening and "disquieting news."[3] Hagar is told, "Return to your mistress and humble yourself," but she is also promised that her descendants will be multiplied. Hagar, like Abraham, receives a promise from God, a promise that her child will father a nation. Clinging to that promise, Hagar obeyed the angelic command and returned to her mistress.

In Genesis 21, Sarah has already given birth to Isaac, but a new worry now weighs on her soul. Sarai fears that Isaac's inheritance will be at risk if Hagar and her son, Ishmael, stay among them. (It is possible that the inheritance Sarah was worried about was also her own dowry should something happen to Abraham.) While we cannot be sure if the inheritance in question was Abraham's or Sarah's, what we do know for certain is that Sarah will not have her son share that inheritance and that she herself will not share equal ranking with a foreign slave. For Sarah, her son's future is at risk, and she must eliminate any threat to his survival and security. Let us remember that Sarah is not selfless in her behavior, because in securing Isaac's future she is also securing her own. And this self interest on Sarah's part marks the beginning of Hagar's journey into despair. Hagar now faces the "pain of displacement and disorientation."[4] Mother and son lose their community (household), find themselves in the wilderness with no water, no food, and no protection from the harsh elements and from bandits; they are aimless and in becoming displaced they have lost home and identity.

This is the second time Hagar has found herself in the desert, only this time the decision was made for her. Years before she had fled her mistress; now she has been banished, forced to dwell in this place of loneliness and death. In the Islamic retelling of this story, called "The Waters of ZamZam," Abraham has sent her away, showing tenderness toward her as he abandoned her to the desert. He tells her that "Allah will provide for you here." While in the desert, Hagar declares to her son, "God will not neglect us."[5] it is interesting to note that in the biblical account, there are no such comforting words from Abraham nor is there a record of Hagar's expression of deep faith in God.

This second frightening desert experience now becomes the means of another encounter between Hagar and God. And as a result of that encounter with God, Hagar and her son not only survive the desert, but she goes on to become the "only woman in the Bible to choose a wife for her son. By choosing a woman from Egypt, she ensures the continuation of her traditions, culture, and values."[6]

Hagar's story has resonated strongly with some African American women. Delores Williams and other womanist scholars have recast the story of Hagar "in the context of the African American woman's historical encounters with slavery."[7] For Williams, as well as for the African American church, emphasis is "put upon God's response to Black people's situation rather than upon what would appear to be hopeless aspects of African American people's existence in North America."[8] In other words, the focus has been upon being able to awaken to God's dreams despite the current situation. By focusing on God's response as the core element that sustains the community of faith, hopelessness and despair can be transformed into hope and expectation. For African American scholar La Verne McCain Gill, the story of Hagar is really a "blueprint for justice." She notes that the Hagar story "introduces patience and faith into the liberation story."[9]

Patience and faith—these two virtues accompany the working of God's justice in our world today. Patience and faith. Can it be that these are the two needed elements that will help awaken us to God's dreams? But let me issue a warning: we are not talking about a passive faith and a frozen patience. We are not talking about sitting in a rocking chair, looking at the clouds and waiting for Jesus to come make things right. This is not what the Hagar-Sarah stories are about. Neither Hagar nor Sarah was passive. Each was a woman of action who made decisions to respond to her life's situation in a particular way. They may have acted without wisdom or without compassion, but they were not passive and there is much to learn about the failures and shortcomings of these decisions. However, the challenge before us still remains: to practice faith and justice as we respond to God's call.

To do the work required by faith is to engage in what liberation theologians from Latin America call praxis. Dietrich Bonhoeffer described this praxis as the "confessional stance of the church in the world."[10] Bonhoeffer says, "The primary confession of the Christian before the world is the deed which interprets itself. . . . The deed alone is our confession of faith before the world."[11] Bonhoeffer reminds us yet again that faith without the deed is no faith at all. We are called to the deed, that is, to our praxis, which is the oxygen of our faith. The theological response to this call to a faith in action leads us to learn to live in true solidarity. Latin American theologian Jon Sobrino defines solidarity as closeness, support, and defense of the weak. He says, "Solidarity is the tenderness of peoples."[12] Listen to this definition one more time: *Solidarity is the tenderness of peoples.* Faith is about doing the hard work of justice, compassion, and loyalty and to do the hard work required of us as we show tenderness toward one another. Patience is about doing the works of faith with perseverance—not giving up, not losing sight that God has dreams for humanity, refusing to give in to fear and despair because we know God will not neglect us.

As a Latina and as an immigrant who came to this country as a child, I find great meaning in the Hagar stories. When I look at Hagar I immediately recognize and identify with her foreignness. I feel for and empathize with that woman whose status as stranger, foreigner, and immigrant makes her vulnerable and powerless. Vulnerable and powerless like the undocumented nannies who come from across the southern border to care for children of wealthy women while they leave their own behind; vulnerable and powerless like the millions of undocumented workers who labor day in and day out across the nation in the low-end jobs found in the hotel and restaurant industries, in lawn and garden services, in meat-packing industries, in the thoroughbred horse farms, in the fields where our food is picked and brought to market. In America we have become afraid of the influx of immigrants. Yet despite our fear of the immigrant, we cannot escape the reality of immigration here in the US and across the globe. According to a United Nations report, 200 million migrants live outside their home countries.13 Will we as Christians continue to react with xenophobia? Will fear of the stranger continue to paralyze our ability to be welcoming? Or will we dare to cultivate the tenderness required of solidarity and work to reform unresponsive immigration policies that will change the lives of so many women and children?

My sisters, the time has come to awaken to God's dreams for humanity, dreams that encompass justice, liberation, healing, and hospitality. I invite you to believe and to act with perseverance, to live in faith and patience. I invite you to begin the courageous act that can be done only by women of faith who are determined to do something about injustice. It is time to awaken to God's dreams and set them in motion, beginning in our own congregations, beginning with our own denominations, beginning in our own homes. It is time to activate the blueprint for transformation and renewal and reconciliation. No one is saying it will be an easy task. No one is saying you will find accolades and applause along the way. But to awaken to God's dreams for humanity—dreams that encompass justice, liberation, healing, and hospitality—will mean that the faith journey we have already begun will take us to new places and change us in radical ways. Are you ready, my sisters? Are you ready to become daughters of the desert? Are you ready to become partners with God in the prophetic task of renewal, reconciliation, and hospitality? Remember Hagar's cry of despair in the wilderness, but also remember her words of great faith, "God will not neglect us."

Amen.

This sermon has been edited for publication. A much longer version, with many more examples, was preached on June 23, 2006, at the Mix in '06 Women's Gathering, held in Indianapolis, Indiana, which brought together more than 4,000 women from the Christian Church (Disciples of Christ) and the United Church of Christ from around the country and across the globe.

1. The Code of Hammurabi, nos. 144–46. http://www.wsu.edu/~dee/MESO/CODE.HTM. Accessed 6/21/06.

2. Sharon Pace Jeansonne, *The Women of Genesis, From Sarah to Potiphar's Wife* (Minneapolis: Fortress Press, 1990),45.

3. Jeansonne, 46.

4. Ibid., 49.

5. Claire Rudolf Murphy, *Daughters of the Desert*(Woodstock, Vt.: Skylight Paths Publishing), 128–29.

6. Jeansonne, 51–2.

7. La Verne McCain Gill, *Daughters of Dignity* (Cleveland: Pilgrim Press, 2000), 15–6.

8. Gill, 19.

9. Ibid.

10. Dennis A. Jacobsen, *Doing Justice: Congregations and Community Organizing* (Minneapolis: Fortress Press, 2001), 94.

11. Jacobsen, 95.

12. Jon Sobrino, "Redeeming Globalization through Its Victims," in *Concilium 2001/5, Globalization and Its Victims,* ed. Jon Sobrino and Felix Wilfred (London: SCM Press, 2001), 111.

13. "Immigration Facts and Fiction," *Newsweek,* International ed., www.msnbc.com (accessed June 21, 2006).

2

Enough Is Enough!¹

Gina M. Stewart

GENESIS 29

She conceived again, and when she gave birth to a son she said, "This time I will praise the LORD." So she named him Judah. Then she stopped having children. (Genesis 29:35, NIV)

One of my favorite scenes in the movie *What's Love Got to Do with It?* is when Tina Turner runs to a motel after an out-and-out brawl with Ike. Her lips are swollen and bleeding, her hair is disheveled, and she's semi-barefooted. She runs across the parking lot to a motel and says to the desk clerk, "I've got 36 cents and a Mobil card, but if you give me a room for the night, as soon as I am able, I will repay you." That night, according to the movie, was a defining moment in Tina's life. She walked away from a life of physical, emotional, and mental abuse. That night, she walked away from an emotional and psychological prison. When Tina decided she had had enough and decided to say no to an unproductive, unhealthy relationship, she opened the door to a new and exciting chapter in her life. And those of us familiar with Tina's career know that from that night forward, the rest is music history.

When I think about Tina's story, I am reminded of the character in this text, Leah, whose name means "wearied" or "afflicted one." She was the oldest daughter of Laban, the older sister of Rachel, and the first wife of Jacob. Biblical historians imply that Leah was not a pretty sight. The Bible describes her as having delicate or weak eyes. As far as Jacob was concerned, Leah was inferior in attractiveness and personality. But her younger sister, Rachel, whose name means "ewe," female sheep, was Jacob's beloved. Jacob did not keep his love for Rachel a secret; in fact, even though Jacob was married to Leah first, it was Rachel who captured his heart, and Jacob was willing to work for seven years to have her hand in marriage. But at the end of seven years, Laban gave Leah to Jacob as a substitute for Rachel. But Jacob was sprung. He loved Rachel so much that he was willing to work another seven years to get the woman of his choice.

Now the text doesn't tell us whether Leah loved Jacob, but it does imply that Jacob didn't love Leah. The tragedy about Leah's relationship with Jacob was not just that Jacob loved someone else. Jacob should have been free to marry whomever he wanted to marry, and Laban shouldn't have deceived him, but the fact that Laban had to trick Jacob into marrying Leah speaks volumes about Laban's opinion of his oldest daughter. After all, Leah never made the short list for Jacob. She wasn't even on Jacob's radar screen for marriage; it was Laban who orchestrated the marriage. It was customary for the oldest daughter to marry first. But the fact that Laban had to trick Jacob into marrying Leah says a lot. From reading the text, we get the impression that Leah invested a lot of time and mental and emotional energy trying to gain Jacob's affection. And Leah had something that Rachel didn't have. Leah could produce.

The text says that when the Lord saw that Leah was unloved—the King James Version says hated—he opened her womb. And Leah produced sons. Now the fact that God opened Leah's womb is significant. Leah lived in a culture that was unapologetically patriarchal, where the individual value of a woman was shaped by a social structure that sustained and perpetuated male dominance over females. In a culture where the relationship between women and men was one of subjugation, subordination, and domination, women were subordinate to men in power and economically dependent upon them for survival. A woman's redemption was in childbearing, and her worth was attached to whether she could produce. Childbearing was so important that institutions were established, like polygamy and adoption, to preserve a father's name on earth. Brothers married their deceased brother's widow if no sons were born prior to his death to leave an heir for the dead.

But despite the fact that Leah was fertile, Jacob didn't change. Each time she gave birth to a son, the names of her sons were an indication of the cry of her heart toward Jacob. The depth of her pain and expectation is illustrated by the names that Leah gave each of her sons. When Leah gave birth to her first son, she named him Reuben, meaning the "Lord has seen" my misery. She thought, *Surely Jacob will love me now.* She had another son and named him Simeon, which means "because the Lord heard" that I am unloved. She had a third son and named him Levi and said, "Now this time my husband will become attached to me, because I have borne him three sons." But in spite of her hope and expectation, Jacob never heard, never saw, and never connected. Consequently, Leah's emotional dependence upon Jacob robbed her of security and self-worth. Although Leah could produce, Jacob did not appreciate her strengths, because she was not Rachel. Leah suffered a wounded self-esteem. She relied too much on Jacob's estimation and evaluation.

Like Leah, so many of us suffer from wounded self-esteem because of someone else's evaluation of us. Although self-esteem refers to our estimation of our own worth, many of us inherited our initial perception of ourselves from other sources: from the Jacobs and Labans in our lives. We never consulted God about our worth. So we suffer from impaired vision, holes in our soul, insecurity, and mistaken identities. Throughout our lives, other people affected our identity by the way they treated us or spoke to us. Some of us have been coddled and cheered all of our lives; some of us have been berated for imperfections over which we had no control. Some of us were always being compared with someone else and never learned to appreciate our own strengths. We have been tolerated rather than celebrated. We feel we are not good enough because we experienced rejection in primary relationships. Consequently, many of us are not just emotionally fatigued, emotionally empty, and emotionally numb, but we are emotionally dependent, believing that the ongoing presence and nurture of another person is necessary for one's security and self-worth. And Leah was emotionally dependent upon Jacob.

But one day, Leah experienced a defining moment that changed her attitude. One day, Leah decided that enough is enough. The change of attitude changed her focus and reshaped her perspective and inner reality. She realized that she could no longer live her life dependent upon the ongoing nurture and approval of Jacob. By the time Leah gave birth to her fourth son, Jacob no longer consumed her thoughts. Leah had a reality check. She finally realized that she couldn't make Jacob love Leah, but she could love Leah, and most of all, God loved Leah! Somewhere between verse 30 and verse 35, Leah experienced a transformation. She gave birth to another son and a new Leah. With the birth of Judah, her fourth son, she said, "This time I will praise the Lord."

I believe Leah must have said to herself, "I had Reuben, and he didn't see me. I had Simeon, and he didn't hear me. I had Levi, and he wouldn't become attached to me. But I can't worry about Jacob any more. I can't live my life or see myself through Jacob's eyes; I can't be my best self, dependent on Jacob's approval and acceptance. I can't grow as long as I am obsessed with what someone else thinks about me. I cannot experience my potential as long as I keep investing my emotional and mental energy in love-deficient relationships. I can't give myself away trying to measure up to somebody else's idea of what acceptable is." Because sometimes, Jacob does not change. And if Jacob's transformation does not take place, I must experience my own transformation. I believe that Leah must have said to herself, "Jacob may not change, but I can change. He may not see me, he may not hear me, and he won't even try to get to know me. But thank God, God sees me, God hears me, and God has blessed me. And this time I will praise the Lord. I am not going to wait until Jacob accepts me. I am not even going to worry that I am not Rachel. I am going to praise the Lord. Because being loved by God is greater than being loved by Jacob."

Like Leah, many of us have Jacobs in our lives. Jacob doesn't necessarily have to be a husband or a lover or a significant other. Jacob could be any primary person in our life we looked to for affirmation and approval. Jacob is the person whose ongoing presence and nurture we believe is essential for our sense of security and self-worth. But at some point, we have to do what Leah did—and say enough is enough. My value is not determined by anybody else. My worth is not based on what I look like, where I live, or the kind of clothes I wear. My worth and my value come from God. And because my value comes from God, I can praise the Lord. Because God is enough, I am enough, and enough is enough.

There comes a time when we have to decide that enough is enough. There is a freedom that accompanies the reality that I was designed and created for more. I do not have to settle for less. I do not have to participate in my own oppression. I was created to live a life of excellence. I was created for good works that God ordained from the beginning. I am better than this situation, and I can do better. We have to decide that our lives are bigger than our pasts. No matter what my mistakes or my shortcomings, the God I serve will empower me to see not only who I am but also what I am capable of becoming. The God I serve will empower me to get to the point where I can say enough is enough. Enough really is enough! We are more than the clothes we wear, the car we drive, the letters behind our name, the titles that we wear, our dress size, or the status we have achieved. God does not love us because of these things; God loves us in spite of these things. In fact, God demonstrated the high value of our lives by giving the life of his Son to die in our place. And that is enough!

A version of this sermon has been preached, with variations, in several places over a number of years, but "Enough Is Enough" was first preached at Berean Baptist Church, in Memphis, Tennessee, for their 2006 Women's Revival.

1. For more prophetic preaching on this and other biblical texts that speak to wounded and abused women, see Elaine Flake, *God in Her Midst: Preaching Healing to Wounded Women,* ed. Kathryn V. Stanley (Valley Forge, PA: Judson Press, 2007).

3

Image or Reality

Helen Bessent Byrd

1 SAMUEL 16:1-13
So he sent and had him brought in. He was ruddy, with a fine appearance and handsome features. Then the LORD said, "Rise and anoint him; he is the one." (1 Samuel 16:12, NIV)

Danzy Senna's short story "Are You Experienced?"[1] describes the struggles of Jo, a fair-skinned, long-haired African American woman. The story begins in 1969. Jo is in a failing marriage to a musician who begins to abuse her. He finally leaves her for another woman, two years after the birth of their child. She visits a friend in New York in order to recover from her failed marriage and has a fling with the famed Jimi Hendrix. But she returns to her husband and son, has another child with him, and resumes life in an abusive relationship. In order to cope, she daydreams about Hendrix and looks for signs in her daughter's face that the child belongs not to her husband but to her lover. She wants to see what is not there.

Like Jo, oftentimes we try so hard to see what we want to see that we deny what is real and opt for our imagination. Today's Scripture lesson from 1 Samuel describes a similar situation. First Samuel 16:6-13 describes David's anointing by Samuel. In the text, Jesse denies, by omission, his youngest son David's existence. God sends Samuel to identify and anoint the future king. Only when he is called out does Jesse identify his son David for Samuel's consideration. Jesse focuses on his tall and handsome oldest son, Eliab. He presents all his sons for consideration, except David, who is left in the fields tending sheep. Jesse dreams of his tall, strong, older son as king, what kings look like. But little David, the shepherd boy?

Frequently, we also are guilty of painting the picture as we wish or expect it to be. We are dreamers and get wrapped up in the way we imagine things would be and don't see them as they are. We deny because sometimes it's difficult to face reality. In psychology, denial is a defense mechanism. When faced with a painful fact, we will reject reality, despite what may be overwhelming and irrefutable evidence. So we envision life as we wish it were by denying what is. It's a human tendency. But reality requires at least three things: recognition, acceptance, and habituation so that we may more nearly approximate the mind of Christ.

When Samuel visits Jesse to choose a king from among Jesse's sons, Jesse moves from denial to recognition. After Samuel questions him regarding whether he has any more sons, Jesse recognizes that he has omitted David from consideration—denying David's possibility of being selected and anointed king. Jesse lies by omission. As Jesse's first son, Eliab, stands before Samuel, Samuel looks on him and thinks, "This is the one." But God warns Samuel not to look at appearance or stature. Samuel was looking but not seeing. Samuel needs a God perspective so he will look beyond the surface. God sees differently from humans, who are satisfied with attention to external factors. The Lord sees inwardly, sees the heart. God sees David's character and concludes that David is a man after God's own heart (1 Samuel 13:14). David is anointed and receives God's Spirit for his role as a leader.

Jesse moves from recognizing David, to seeing him as God does, to acceptance. He moves from what is expected, from the notion that the oldest child ought to be chosen, to accept God's choice, which is beyond what society expects. As we are faced with our fantasy or reality, we are forced to choose between denial and acceptance. We have an opportunity to agree with God, to change our perception.

Jesse is in denial because he does not consider that David, the shepherd boy, could be king. David doesn't have what it takes. He doesn't have a king's stature or maturity in Jesse's estimation. Only when Samuel identifies David as the future king does Jesse accept that not his first son but his eighth son will become king. He agrees with God's plan; he becomes God's ally. Like Jesse, we ally with God by accepting God's ordained visions rather than our own imaginations.

Once we come out of denial and accept God's view, we are called to develop the habit of living in that reality. Habit, repetitious behavior that becomes easy, helps us grow in our Christian living. Habit helps us acclimate to unchanging environmental conditions; it helps us become sensitized or accustomed to the milieu in which we function.

In today's Bible story, we do not know whether Jesse changed his mental attitude from denial to recognition to acceptance. But as he receives the revelation that David will be the next king, I believe he assumes the challenge, as we do, to make a habit of looking deeper. Maybe he practices seeing more about all of his sons. When we make a good practice a habit, it matures us.

If this text teaches us anything, it teaches us that old proverb that "you can't judge a book by its cover" is true. We can't focus on the package. With God, appearance doesn't count. But perceptions can and do change, and we are called to embrace God's vision, depth of seeing. We are called to accept it and make seeing from God's point of view a habit. And, thank God, we can. Amen.

A version of this sermon was preached at Covenant Presbyterian Church, Norfolk, Virginia, in October 2007.

1. Danzy Senna, "Are You Experienced?" in *Gumbo: An Anthology of African American Writing*, ed. E. Lynn Harris and Marita Golden (New York: Broadway Books, 2002).

4

The Silence We Keep

MarQuita A. Carmichael Burton

2 SAMUEL 13:19-20

But Tamar put ashes on her head, and tore the long robe that she was wearing; she put her hand on her head, and went away, crying aloud as she went. Her brother Absalom said to her, "Has Amnon your brother been with you? Be quiet for now, my sister; he is your brother; do not take this to heart." So Tamar remained, a desolate woman, in her brother Absalom's house. (2 Samuel 13:19-20, NRSV)

My dear friends, in the passage before us, Absalom counsels his sister Tamar, King David's daughter. Tamar's brother Amnon forcefully rapes her in her father's house. Absalom sees his flesh and blood, his sister, in the worst condition of her life. She has been violated in the house of the king: a place one might assume offers safety and protection for women in a patriarchal society since protecting women's sexual property was important in a male-dominated society. She is bruised and humiliated. She tears her princess garment to announce that something terrible has happened to her. Her brother Absalom's salve is to tell her to keep silent.

Absalom asks for Tamar's silence and expects it. She gives it because that's what women in her society did: they bowed to the will of men, even to their own hurt. Like our sister Tamar, we often keep silent about sexual abuses we suffered in childhood; we mute our own existence in an effort to avoid exposing our families to public humiliation. African Americans, especially, often place great value on the group, our "skin and kin,"[1] rather than those who support us individually. We have often given higher priority to our elders' desires to keep secrets or keep peace than to getting help we desperately need in order to be healed.

As black and brown people, we often ignore trauma inflicted on the very people we profess to love when we try to avoid revealing sexual crimes committed against us by our own clan members. Our women and children—boys and girls—become expendable when what the group wants supersedes the healing of the unprotected. Survivors of sexual assault often will keep silent, even as adults, in an effort not to be a burden or blame for a family's dysfunction. Tamar keeps silent to honor Absalom's request and to protect Amnon's status. But her silence does not protect her.

As we maintain our silence even as adults, we may find ourselves living in fear and self-imposed isolation, unable to trust people. Tamar closes off, desolate, in Absalom's house. She separates from the king's other children and succumbs to isolation. One of the casualties when we keep sexual crime secrets is our capacity to receive and to give love. In our culture, the responses of victims range from promiscuity on one end to abstinence from physical contact on the other. It's the cost we pay if we do not receive the help we need to know the truth that we are not at fault, we did not invite the abuse, and we did not deserve the violence. And our silence often shows in our bodies: post-traumatic stress disorders, psychological challenges, and overall poor health and self-esteem, Tamar's desolation in twenty-first-century garb.

We may be well-off, singing, or on welfare, struggling. It doesn't matter. If we create sacred spaces for our beloved babies, then look away while they are being sexually assaulted, we become like silent partners in a gang rape; our silence signals consent. We become Absalom, demanding silence. Generations suffer wounds of the heart and mind that the body cannot easily expel. Our communities and households will lose great thinkers, dreamers, preachers, artists, daughters, and sons because of psychological and spiritual damage inflicted on them in nests defiled by incest, molestation, and sexual violence. If we do not change course, perpetrators will be free to abuse more children; the cycle of violence, unchecked, will continue; millions of our clan and tribe will suffer silently and not get the help they need to be restored to wholeness.

Perhaps Absalom is so entrenched in his culture that he cannot imagine the desolation silence brings on Tamar. Perhaps he cannot imagine how his words, "he is your brother," minimize her pain. Or maybe the revenge he plans consumes him. Either way, his advice and Amnon's despicable deed become the actions that help destroy Tamar, David's family, and a nation. Since we see how sexual assault and violence can devastate, we must no longer consent to the power of silence. It is spoken truth that will make us free. I believe we must collectively confess with Sister Audre Lorde that "our silence cannot save us" and reclaim our voices. "There is no way to speak and do the truth in an oppressive society without offending the people who are responsible for that oppression," and since "there comes a time when our silence is betrayal,"[2] we trade in our torn robes and ashes for a bullhorn and a listening ear and tell our stories so our souls, minds, bodies, and the people we say we love may be healed.

Tamar lived in patriarchal times, in a life situation far different from our lives today. Our response to sexual violence in intimate relationships does not have to be the same as hers. Tamar's community forced her to carry guilt and shame; it forced her to live her life as a desolate woman living in her brother Absalom's house. But her plight does not have to be our present reality. As the daughter of the king, Tamar's options were limited, but as honored and beloved children of God, our options can be very different.

The first step we may consider in our quest for restoration of our best selves is to understand that we cannot wait for someone else to rescue and heal us. We must begin that work on our own. An honest, critical evaluation of who we are, and how we have become who we are, leads to our self-reconciliatory work. Writing our stories down helps us revisit fearful and tearful places. We can write without retribution every violation, every time, every name; we can reveal our true stories and release them from the places in our bodies where we've hidden them. We can reclaim whatever we have torn and whatever has been stripped from us. My sisters and brothers, we can shatter the façade of safety in silence with the first stroke of our pens. Tell the story.

When we accept what we find as we tell our stories, we free ourselves from the silences we have kept. Once we tell the story and write it down, once we tell someone in authority, we can no longer pretend "as if this true story never happened."[3] We must press on even if we have to cry the whole way through. An African proverb warns that people who conceal their illness cannot expect to be healed. If we consent to stay quiet about our abuses and violent life disruptions, we cannot expect to truly enter into wholeness.

Survivors of sexual violence, silent no more, will need support. Not support that leads to desolation, but counselors, professional healers, who may help us find God's grace. We will need support from friends and family who can help us mend the torn garments of our lives. We will need safety, a nest, and a listening ear, with a heart that speaks truth.

Finally, we must embrace the holiness and sacredness of loving ourselves by connecting to spiritual truths like those found in Baby Sugg's prayer and blessing for the people in Toni Morrison's *Beloved*: "She told them that the only grace they could have was the grace they could imagine. . . . 'Here,' she said, 'in this here place, we flesh; flesh that weeps, laughs, flesh that dances on bare feet in grass. Love it. Love it hard. . . . More than your life-holding womb and your life-giving private parts hear me now, love your heart. For this is the prize.'"[4]

This sermon was preached in a workshop at the National Cathedral College of Preachers held in Washington, DC, in spring 2007.

1. Katie G. Cannon, in a personal consultation at the Women of Color Preaching Festival, College of Preachers, Washington National Cathedral, May 2007.

2. James H. Cone, "The Vocation of a Theologian," *Union News* (Winter 1991): 3.

3. Katie G. Cannon, "As If This True Story Never Happened." A presentation given at the Miles Jerome Jones Institute on Preaching and Community Concern, May 13, 2004, Virginia Union University.

4. Toni Morrison, "From Beloved," 102–4, in *My Soul Is a Witness: African American Women's Spirituality,* Gloria Wade-Gayles, ed. (Boston: Beacon Press, 1995), 104.

5

Wash and Be Cleansed!

Christine Y. Wiley

2 KINGS 5:1-14

So he went down and immersed himself seven times in the Jordan, according to the word of the man of God; his flesh was restored like the flesh of a young boy, and he was clean. (2 Kings 5:14, NRSV)

"And he was clean." When we hear this phrase, various things may come to mind. We may think of dirt on our bodies. We bathe regularly and wash our hair and brush our teeth so that we can rid ourselves of any external dirt and grime. Then we have our internal selves. We want our thoughts to be clean. As we take Holy Communion, we examine the essence of who we are. Are we living a clean life that would please God? We think about whether we are whole, whether we are pure, whether we are clean.

In our story today, Naaman was an important man, the commander of the army of Aram. He wanted to be clean. He wanted to be without disease, to be cured, to be healed from the dreaded leprosy. Some of us might immediately know of areas in our lives that need to be cleaned up. Others may think of something as I preach. But I admonish all of us to take time to look at places in our lives where we feel we are not clean or whole.

Perhaps our past haunts us, and we are not living a healthy and effective life because we can't get over our past. Or maybe we are gripped in fear. Sometimes fear will not allow us to live authentic lives, and we find ourselves wearing a mask and not trusting the world around us. Maybe we don't have the confidence to claim that we have what it takes to live an abundant life.

Is it pride that we struggle with? Are we fighting addictions? Or maybe we are like so many who have the legacy of slavery in this country—we just feel unclean. Our experiences and our history leave us feeling unworthy. No matter how good we are, or how nice we try to be, we feel as if God just couldn't forgive us or accept us. Let us take a good look at Naaman's story.

> Naaman, commander of the army of the king of Aram, was a great man and in high favor with his master, because by him the LORD had given victory to Aram. The man, though a mighty warrior, suffered from leprosy. Now the Arameans on one of their raids had taken a young girl captive from the land of Israel, and she served Naaman's wife. She said to her mistress, "If only my lord were with the prophet who is in Samaria! He would cure him of his leprosy." So Naaman went in and told his lord just what the girl from the land of Israel had said. (2 Kings 5:1-4, NRSV)

It is interesting that the writer of this story says that the Lord, the God of Israel, gave military success to Naaman. Naaman was not a worshiper of God or an Israelite. As a matter of fact, the Arameans and the Israelites had a confusing relationship. They went back and forth in their squabbles and raids on each other. Israel's enemies were thought to be victorious because of God's intervention. Why would God give favor to someone who was not one of the children of God, as the Israelites understood a child of God? The fact of the matter is that God gives favor to some other people. People who are marginalized, people who are different, people whom we have judged find themselves in God's presence and favor. Some in this country love to say, "God bless America!" But God will bless whomever God wants to bless, whether human beings feel those particular people are worthy or not.

Naaman had the dreaded skin disease called leprosy. There was no cure for it. It seemed to be in the very early stages for him, but he was concerned and afraid. I imagine that it was similar to the 1980s with the advent of AIDS. There was no cure and no treatment. Today leprosy is called Hansen's disease. The Centers for Disease Control and Prevention describe this disorder as an ailment that causes deterioration of the skin and ligaments that hold the joints together. Untreated, this disease is fatal.[1] Because of a faithful God, today there is treatment that can cure leprosy. And I believe that we will also watch a faithful God bring forth a cure for diseases that affect our community such as sickle cell anemia, diabetes, cancer, kidney disease, and AIDS. At the time in which Naaman lived, people who had leprosy were given a death sentence. As the disease progressed, the people would be banned from the city to live together in the outskirts of town. If you walked from one place to another and there was a person with leprosy nearby, that person had to warn everyone by shouting, "Unclean! Unclean!" But there are some steps we can take to be cleansed.

The first thing one must do to be clean is to be humble. God took a humble servant, a girl, a foreigner, an Israelite, and used her. Ironically, Naaman's only hope of being cured came from Israel, came from a young girl. Isn't that just like God? The very persons we may find ourselves not paying much attention to, looking down upon, or not valuing are the very people God will use to bring forth our healing and a sense of wholeness.

Naaman would not ordinarily have listened to a slave, a girl, an Israelite, but he wanted to be clean. No matter how humble we believe our position in life is, God can use anyone to spread God's message. I dare any one of us to be open to be used by God like this Israelite girl. When we want to be clean, when we want to be delivered, we just want it to happen. We don't care who helps us. God will humble us and allow us to realize that sometimes the only way God can get our attention is to send us a problem we can't handle.

Second, to be made clean, we must listen for God. Perhaps there was something about this young servant girl that pointed to God. She was not only a witness to the true and living God, but also she pointed Naaman to his healing. Sometimes we predetermine how God may communicate with us. We miss God because we are not in a listening mode. God will speak to us through our circumstances, through worship, through the Bible, and, yes, through people. We must open our eyes and our hearts.

Because of the young girl's testimony, the Aramean king sends a letter and gifts to the Israelite king with a request for a cure for Naaman. In the midst of the Israelite king's panic at such a request, Elisha the

23

prophet said, "Send Naaman to me." Naaman went to Elisha's house after Elisha sent for him and drove up in style with all his horses and chariots. He came with pomp and circumstance. He had no humility; he did not have open ears and an open heart to listen for God. Naaman, in all his robes, expected the man of God to come out to personally greet him, stand up majestically, for all to see, and say he spoke for God. And then he wanted Elisha to dramatically wave his hands over the diseased spot, and behold, he would be made clean! But no, instead, Elisha the prophet—Elisha, the one who took over from Elijah and asked for a double portion of his spirit; Elisha, the compassionate expert in taking care of people, the one proficient in pastoral care—sent his servant out to greet Naaman. He did not come out himself but gave a message for Naaman to immerse himself seven times in the River Jordan for a healing.

This scene was not the way that Naaman had envisioned it! The answer was nothing like he thought it would be. Naaman was full of pride. Whatever humility he had went straight out of the window. He wasn't listening anymore! He was asked to immerse himself in the dirty Jordan River when he had cleaner rivers back home. It didn't sound right to him. It did not sound spiritual enough or important enough. Therefore he said, "I'm outta here!"

Perhaps Naaman didn't understand the role of the prophet. Marvin McMickle, in *Where Have All the Prophets Gone?*[2] reminds us that Old Testament prophets were to sound the alarm about injuries and injustice. They were to teach and guide. That is what the church is to do today. They spoke truth to power. They took a risk and were obedient to share.

When Naaman received word back from Elisha, once again it was marginalized persons who got his attention. Two servants humbled him and made him listen. These servants—perhaps no one would look at or listen to them—said, "If the prophet had asked you to do something hard and heroic, wouldn't you have done it? So why not this simple 'wash and be clean'?" Naaman was humbled by the least of these, the marginalized. He finally humbled himself, and he listened. He dropped his proud defenses and bathed in the dirty water as he was told to do.

Finally, then, the third thing that Naaman needed to do to be made clean was to obey. He obeyed and was made clean, cured of his leprosy. He humbled himself and heard God's wisdom in a servant girl and his two servant companions. He took a risk, humbled himself, listened, and obeyed God.

We are not to find ourselves so caught up in our own situations that we cannot address what is going on in our world. The more we are able to address the evils in our communities, the better we will be able to heal and cleanse our own issues. How are we responding to homelessness, immigration, incarceration, and poverty? Wonderful praise and worship in our churches is not enough. We must humble ourselves and listen for opportunities to bring cleansing in the form of justice and righteousness to our communities. We must critique ourselves when there are certain issues that we don't want to hear. The word of God is a radical word. If we listen, God will speak and will use others to challenge us, cleanse us, and heal us.

Do we want to be clean today? Do we want to bring a cleansing word to our world? Stop looking down on anyone or anything. Let's humble ourselves. Let's listen and know that we might not like the way that God is directing us because of our self-centeredness, but if we proceed with obedience, we will be washed and made clean.

> Consider your own call, brothers and sisters: not many of you were wise by human standards, not many were powerful, not many were of noble birth. But God chose what is foolish in the world to shame the wise; God chose what is weak in the world to shame the strong; God chose what is low and despised in the world, things that are not, to reduce to nothing things that are. (1 Corinthians 1:26-28, NRSV)

Naaman thought he only needed his leprosy cured, but God washed him and cleansed him not only of his disease, but also of his rebellious and prideful heart. We, too, will be cleansed if we humble ourselves, if we listen, and if we are obedient. But it is not our definition of cleansing, but God's. Don't be afraid to be cleansed!

Come on down to the river with me, and in our Baptist tradition, be totally immersed.

Once—don't worry that we aren't used to this kind of water, we're starting to feel better already, aren't we? Twice—don't be afraid to go down all the way, we're starting to look better! Three times—look! The oozing of our sores has stopped! Four times—we are so wet, now we want to do what God wants us to do, we desire the Holy Spirit!

Five times—the filth is coming off, we are praying for those who lie in our faces, those who despitefully use us and talk about us. We are asking God to help us love better! Six times—we are changed. Our past doesn't haunt us anymore. We are washed and made new. The dirt is gone. Seven times—seven means completion, perfection, and seven symbolizes the Spirit of God. But wait a minute, this seventh immersion is no longer immersion in muddy water; it is the blood of Jesus!

We have an invitation that Naaman didn't have—to come and be washed in the blood of Jesus! "For the message of the cross is foolishness to those who are perishing, but to us who are being saved it is the power of God" (1 Corinthians 1:18, NRSV). Jump in; it will heal us, cleanse us and deliver us. Salvation is ours. Deliverance is ours. Cleansing is ours. Wash and be cleansed!

A version of this sermon was preached on July 8, 2007, at Covenant Baptist Church, Washington, D.C.

1. Hansen's disease (leprosy), Centers for Disease Control and Prevention, http://www.cdc.gov/ncidod/dbmd/diseaseinfo/hansens_htm (accessed July 2007).

2. Marvin McMickle, *Where Have All the Prophets Gone? Reclaiming Prophetic Preaching in America* (Cleveland: Pilgrim Press, 2006).

6
Hell No!

Melva L. Sampson

ESTHER 1:1-12
But Queen Vashti refused to come at the king's command conveyed by the eunuchs. (Esther 1:12, NRSV)

> Girl child ain't safe in a family o' mens.
> Sick 'n tired how a woman still live like a slave.
> You better learn how to fight back while you still alive . . .
> But he try to make me mind and I just ain't that kind . . .
> Hell No!
> —From "Hell No!" *The Color Purple,* the musical

Around my big momma's kitchen table, where green beans were snapped and the daily rumor mill was spun, the phrase "Hell no!" signaled an emphatic refusal used to express discontent toward a person, place, or thing. While the saved, sanctified, and filled with the Holy Ghost folk considered the phrase profane and not fit for Christians, especially women, in Nez's kitchen, as we affectionately called it, "Hell no!" was a saying of righteous indignation, the opposite of blasphemy but an acknowledgment of the reverence for ourselves as wholly holy and without restraint to resist whatever sought to silence our voices. "Hell no!" was sho' nuff grown woman's talk. When uttered, one could visualize the exclamation point that followed in the form of cutting eyes, between hissed teeth, and spewing from pursed lips. Women in my family sat around the kitchen table reclaiming, reviving, and revolutionizing black women's roles in church and society. When asked if she would "honor and obey" during one of her three wedding ceremonies, my big momma, Nez, said, "Hell no!" When the pastor summoned my mother to ask her to consider staying with my father, even though he was physically and verbally abusive, my mother responded with a resounding, "Hell no!" When asked if I would preach from the floor because the pulpit was reserved for male authority, I looked the deacon square in the eye and vehemently replied, "Hell no!"

When I read Vashti's story, I think of Nez, who, if she had been with Vashti after hearing the king's request, surely would have looked at the queen and given her the royal nod to repeat after her and say, "Hell no!"

The story recorded in Esther opens by describing a lavish party sponsored by King Ahasureus. The 180-day shindig celebrated the king's recent conquests. To top off his excessive display of wealth, the king sponsored an even more extravagant 7-day affair for all of the citizens of Susa. Drunk with wine and out of toys to display, the king decided to go for the shock-and-awe factor. He summoned Queen Vashti to appear at the party immediately, adorned, as some would suggest, with only her royal crown. The text reads, "But Queen Vashti refused to come at the king's command conveyed by the eunuchs. At this the king was enraged and his anger burned within him." Vashti was banished from the kingdom and ordered never to come before the king again. Her crown would be given to another who would be better than she.

Queen Vashti's response often is overlooked for the more palatable story of Esther. Yet to gloss over this monumental moment of liberation is to miss the making of a model of leadership in which following the sound of the genuine[1] within one's self is paramount. Such a model moves us from the sin of self-sacrifice and self-abnegation to the virtues of self-acceptance and self-development. Vashti's metaphorical response of "hell no!" became a model for all the women in Susa and a threat to those who would have found pleasure in her debasing display. The price she paid for dissing the king was dear—banishment. Yet, I imagine it was only a small price to pay for retrieving her voice, dignity, and worth. Vashti's insistence on taking care of herself reveals to us that we too will be faced with life-altering decisions when we decide to honor our own divinity. Vashti's actions and the king's response are telltale signs that we, too, will have to choose between revolution and apathy, between objectification and humanization, and between the inevitability of pain and the option of misery. We will all one day be summoned to the king and be forced to choose between a mealy-mouthed yes and an emphatic "Hell no!" The cost of living within the empire had become too great. Exile was yet a light affliction in exchange for her ability to answer the call to her own integrity and freedom. Her story provides us with three points to ponder.

First, Vashti's response reveals that we should beware of the invitations we entertain. As in the queen's case, we can rest assured that at some point in time we will be summoned to come before the king and in some cases bearing only our royal crown. We will be called to stand before the intellectually impotent and the spiritually bankrupt. We must beware of the invitations we entertain so as not to fall victim to a false sense of promotion that stems from our need to be recognized. Every invitation is not worth accepting and should be scrutinized thoroughly, or we too will be put in the position of appearing naked before the king's court.

Second, we must beware of the pride of the powerful. The pride of the king was fueled on the perceived powerlessness of Vashti. In the musical *The Color Purple,* adapted from the Pulitzer Prize–winning novel by Alice Walker and the film by Steven Spielberg, the character Sofia and her sisters sing and dance their way into a spiritual frenzy as they respond to Harpo's pride, the alleged powerful, with a loud "Hell no!" When we respond to our voice, we threaten the pride of the powerful. We must learn how to fight back in ways that annihilate both the pride and the power of those who seek to enslave our bodies, minds, and souls. The pride of the powerful is fueled by our silence. It desires to keep us beholden to weak-willed, fickle, and self-centered people. The pride of the powerful thrives on complete control and seeks to conquer our inner psyche, which if successful can ultimately thwart our inner ability to say, "Hell no!"

Third, we need to beware of false thrills; outward success is not equal to inner worth. Vashti was groomed to give the appearance of outward success. Being chosen as queen was a sign of successful training. Vashti's story is symbolic of struggles we face as we seek to assert ourselves in contexts where we are expected to submit and care only about others. Carol Lakey Hess cautions that had the queen disregarded her own feelings and submitted to the will of the king, she would have lost herself ever so quietly. She notes, "No one would have noticed; she would have simply colluded with quiet conspiracy."[2] The moral to Vashti's refusal is simple—outward success is not equal to inner worth. Material gain, position, and status are never worth giving one's soul away.

In a scene in the movie *The Color Purple*, the mayor and his wife approach Sofia. The couple is portrayed as somewhat liberal in a time when racism was excessive and flagrant. Miss Millie, the mayor's wife, asks Sofia if she wants to come and be her maid. Sofia's response is classic: "Hell no!" Astonished at her response, the mayor asks, "What did you say, gal?" Sofia responds again, "Hell no!" A verbal argument ensues and then a physical altercation. The crowd violently subdues Sofia in front of her children and takes her off to jail, where she spends many years. When she is released, she is sent to work for Miss Millie after all. After she completes her time with Miss Millie, she dines with her family. At the dinner table she reclaims her muted voice, recounts the reason for her response, and celebrates the sound of her own voice—the sound of the genuine. The stories of Sofia, Vashti, and women around Nez's table reveal a profound question.

When is the last time you said, "Hell no"? Esther resolved, "If I perish let me perish." Fannie Lou Hamer proclaimed, "I'm sick and tired of being sick and tired." Our great elder Maya Angelou penned, "And Still I Rise." Sister Shange shouted, "I found God in myself and I loved her/I loved her fiercely." Anna Julia Cooper said soundly, "When and where I enter, the whole race enters with me." God rejoices when we acknowledge the sound of our own voices. It is when we find our voices that we celebrate who God created us to be. These women paid high prices for freeing themselves from male authority, patriarchal dominance, and humiliating roles. Yet their responses suggest that more times than not we need to say, "Hell no!" Sometimes, a simple answer of "No," "No thank you," or "I'm sorry, I'll pass" just doesn't get it. We need to go for the shock-and-awe value and retrieve our voice, our power, and our bodies. As the song in the musical urges, "We have to learn how to respond while we're still alive." What will you do when the king/queen comes for you?

A version of this sermon was preached at First African Presbyterian Church, June 2007.

1. Howard Thurman, "The Sound of the Genuine," 1980 baccalaureate address, Spelman College, Sisters Chapel. Thurman explains this sound as the authentic voice within everyone, the voice that beckons us to be true to the divinity within.

2. Carol Lakey Hess, *Caretakers of Our Common House: Women's Development in Communities of Faith* (Nashville: Abingdon, 1997), 44.

Gambling with God

Lisa Wilson Davison

JOB 2:1-10

"But stretch out your hand now and touch his bone and flesh, and he will curse you to your face." The LORD said to Satan, "Very well; he is in your power; only spare his life." (Job 2:5-6, NRSV)

My sophomore year of college I took a course in psychology to fulfill my lab science requirement for the liberal arts curriculum. When I found out that psychology could be done in place of biology or chemistry, I was thrilled. In the second part of class, we studied animal behavior. We were each assigned a white rat. Now, if you had told me prior to that class that I could become attached to a rodent, I would have thought you were crazy. But that rat became my pet. I don't remember what I named her, so we'll just call her Gracie. It was amazing to watch this small animal learn new tricks. I'm sad to report that at the end of the semester, Gracie and all the other rats were taken to the biology lab and fed to the snakes. I was heartbroken. Death by snake seemed like an unfair destiny for Gracie. I had trained her. But later I realized she wasn't trying to please me; she only wanted the food, the prize.

Ten years later, I taught a pre-ministry class as chaplain of Culver-Stockton College. The topic for the day was evangelism, and we wandered onto a tangential path of discussing salvation. One of the members, I will call him Chuck, had been reared in a fundamentalist, evangelical church. He was not shy about speaking his mind. As I presented the class with a few ways people view salvation, I spoke about those who believed that everyone is saved, regardless of their religious faith or lack thereof, and despite their actions in this life. As I expected, one of the students asked the usual question: Does that mean Hitler is in heaven? I carefully tried to explain to them this view of God, which happens to be my own. Chuck raised his hand and said the inevitable: "Well, if everyone gets to heaven, why should I worry with being good?"

Now, I do not mean to pick on Chuck. He was not the first to make such a statement, and I believe a majority of Christians hold his view of faith, the ever-present reward-punishment view of why we are to be faithful. People have used this understanding as a fear tactic to convert people to Christianity for centuries. If you don't believe in Jesus, you're going to hell. If you do believe in Jesus, you get to go to heaven. I shudder to think of all the revival conversions that have taken place throughout history based solely on the threat of punishment. But, to be honest, Christians did not come up with this kind of reward-punishment understanding of the world all on our own. While emphasis on conversion and the afterlife is unique to Christian evangelists, there are plenty of places in the First Testament from which you can reach a "reap what you sow" theology.

This theology dominates the books of Joshua through Chronicles, where we see the Israelites reflecting on their history and trying to explain, from their faith perspective, why things happened the way they did. Without a belief in some sort of afterlife, people experienced rewards and punishments in this life. Since the Israelites were monotheistic, that is, they worshiped only one God, they could not blame bad things that happened on another god or the devil. In fact, the idea of a devil figure, a supernatural being that works against God, did not develop until after the books of the Jewish Bible were written. The *ha-satan* in Job refers to a member of God's heavenly court who works for God to determine a human being's faithfulness. In the opening chapters of Job, we see that *ha-satan* freely comes and goes in God's presence. I like to think of *ha-satan* as God's district attorney or consigliere. A consigliere, as you may know, means a counselor or advisor; popularly, it means the person who advises the crime boss in syndicated crime rings.

When faced with the tragedies of being conquered by foreign enemies, the exile, and the destruction of the temple, the Israelites looked for where they went wrong. These tragic events were seen as punishment for being unfaithful to God. Likewise, their bright spots in history were seen as rewards for their getting it right. Beyond Joshua through Chronicles, the book of Proverbs and some of the Psalms draw similar conclusions: "The LORD watches over the way of the righteous, but the way of the wicked will perish" (Psalm 1:6, NRSV).

This view of life did not always satisfy the Israelites. For one thing, not every bad experience could be traced to a wrong deed. Also, the destruction of the temple and the loss of the Promised Land seemed like too harsh a punishment for anything the Israelites could have done. From these thoughts and experiences, a different voice emerged and took canonical form, a voice that threatened the traditional wisdom of "you reap what you sow." This voice is found in the book of Ecclesiastes. Here we find a view of the world that proclaims God is present and somehow in control but also knows that the easy rules for life are insufficient. The conclusion: worship God, do your best, and enjoy life while you can.

Another version of this divergent voice is found in the book of Job. Despite what many people would like to think, this text is not about suffering in silence. All one has to do is read Job 3–42, and one will see that Job was anything but silent or patient. This book is much more about wrestling with the question of unexplained suffering. The writers in exile in Babylon, influenced by other cultures' stories of a righteous sufferer, developed a folktale, infused with poetry, to counterbalance the dominant "you reap what you sow" message.

But I also think that their final product did more than present the message that innocent people suffer. The book of Job provides an important message about why we are faithful. It confronts those who are being good only to get the reward at the end of the maze of life. Clearly, we see in Job an image of someone who remains faithful despite the lack of rewards.

Beyond this message, the story of Job makes an important statement about God. How on earth, you might ask? In fact, I've had many students tell me that they just can't swallow this picture of God. Surely a just and righteous God would not allow, or cause, someone to suffer just to see if that person is faithful or not. How cruel! Now, I'm the first to admit that the image of God presented in this biblical text is very troubling, especially in Job 1–2. Let's face it. No one wants to imagine God sitting in heaven gambling with our lives in some celestial game of chance. Yet I believe that in order to glean from this story another view of God, we must read it properly. The character of God in this folktale is based in a different culture with its own understandings of how the world worked. Job, we must remember, is a story and not a biography; thus, the authors were not making the claim that these events actually happened. If we immerse ourselves in Job as story, then we get a different perspective.

In the context of the story, God does not know how Job will behave. This is not the all-knowing God many envision, who knows what human beings will do before we even act. No, God must wait to see how Job will respond to the calamities that fall upon him. This understanding reminds us that God's taking on the *ha-satan*'s challenge to see what kind of faith Job has is truly a risk on God's part. There is a chance God could lose. Yet God takes the bet anyway. And, according to the story, God wins the bet. Job never does curse God or lose his faith in God. It would appear that God takes the bet with the *ha-satan* expecting to win, and God does. Despite what the *ha-satan* thinks, God has faith in Job that Job can be faithful just because that's what God asks of him and not in order to get any kind of reward.

As a folktale, the book of Job is meant to be read not only as a story about one person but also in a more global way. That is, we the readers are to understand that, in this story, Job represents all humanity; he represents us. Thus, the implied message is that not only does God have faith in Job, but also God has faith in us. God believes we can be faithful and make good choices because God asks that of us and not just to get a reward—be that material blessings in this life or a heavenly reward. Some might say that God's creation of humanity and God's choice to give us power to make our own choices was risky from the beginning. It was a gamble, but thanks be to God, our God is willing to take chances on us!

A version of this sermon was preached on October 12, 2003, at Kaleidoscope Disciples of Christ Church in Lexington, Kentucky.

8

Is God in the Dungeon?

E. Anne Henning Byfield

PSALM 139:7-12

Where can I go from your spirit? Or where can I flee from your presence?
(Psalm 139:7, NRSV)

Where Are You God?

where are you God?
when evil is aggravating
people are agitating
daughter in Iraq
government corrupt
can't get a job
my man's downlow
drugs/diseases overflow
violence is choking me
hypocrisy is bringing misery,
unfreedom,
injustice
and lack of
equality.
when we are
in pain
sickness
slavery
and death
where are you God?[1]

This question—where are you, God—emerged out of a preaching engagement in 1993 in Accra, Ghana. While there, I visited Cape Elmina Castle, also known as St. George's Castle, on the beautiful coastlands of Ghana. Inside, you can feel the dark presence and spirit of our ancestors, knowing that one of the most horrific acts in history occurred within these walls. This is where Africans were housed, beaten, and thrown in the sea for minor sicknesses before walking the path to the Door of No Return. In the midst of this dreadful place are two church buildings, a Wesleyan church and the Dutch Reformed church. The slave traders worked together but did not worship together. On Sundays, where slaves may not have known one day from the next, they could hear hymns such as "O for a Thousand Tongues to Sing" and "We Gather Together to Ask the Lord's Blessing."

Written on the walls of the Dutch Reformed Church was Psalm 132:13-14: "For the LORD has chosen Zion; he has desired it for his habitation: This is my resting place forever; here I will reside, for I have desired it" (NRSV). While stunned at such an unusual Scripture inside a slave castle, I was more stunned by the words of the curator. With quiet rage, he spoke softly, saying, "God was not in the dungeon." The preacher in me wanted to preach an exegesis on God's presence. The pained African in me did not allow me to speak. I stood there and wept.

Where is God when we face the worst of the worst? Daily we live through the insanity of the war in Iraq and Afghanistan, the continual tragedy for the victims of Hurricane Katrina, molestations, murders, and mayhem. How does one answer this question when one experiences isolation and desolation? With the same quiet rage we wonder, *Is God in the midst of such chaos?*

The quick answers we received as children often do not sustain us as adults. As children, we learned that God is everywhere. We have heard preachers quote, "When you pass through the waters, I will be with you; and through the rivers, they shall not overwhelm you" (Isaiah 43:2, NRSV). We memorized Psalm 23: "Yea, though I walk through the valley of the shadow of death, I will fear no evil: for thou art with me" (v. 4, KJV). Yet these answers do not always satisfy us when we are in despair.

It was Psalm 139 that helped me answer the question "Is God in the dungeon?" In this psalm, God is described as an omniscient and omnipresent God, one who knows and is ever present. That description in itself brings comfort but not always clarity. Formed by the Creator, our thoughts, pains, situations, and triumphs are intimately known by God. Why the writer writes these words is not completely evident, but whatever his circumstances, Psalm 139:1-6 is personally assuring.[2] Yahweh is there, understands, and handles my person and my condition. Whatever dungeon the psalmist had entered, he is secure even in his insecurity that God is on the journey with him.

We also are journeying with the majestic One. The ultimate destination and purpose may not be known to us. The course of our journey may not be immediately understood, but the psalmist is confident and persuaded that God is with us. It does not matter how we get there. What matters is that once there we have the presence of God.

The dungeon experience is not always the result of an external happenstance. In fact, there are three ways we may end up in the dungeon. We can end up in the dungeon by our own sinfulness. Our actions have a causal consequence of separation and isolation. If we believe that sin is separation from God, the heaviness of our behavior often places us in emotional exile and estrangement.

Dungeons will also come by external assaults when something or someone causes the pain we are facing. Often it comes quickly, without any warning. These external assaults include drive-by shootings, car accidents, domestic violence, and unfair job losses. Their action causes our tumultuous reaction.

The third way we may find ourselves in the dungeon is when God pushes us into the wilderness: "You hem me in, behind and before, and lay your hand upon me" (Psalm 139:5, NRSV). For whatever reason, God does not just allow the suffering; God orchestrates and navigates us into the dungeon. There is a divine intentionality. It may be for our growth, healing, or some other known or unknown purpose. Abraham is told by God to sacrifice his son (Genesis 22:1-19). Rizpah had to lose her son for a political war and then fight to get a decent burial (2 Samuel 21:10-14). Who can completely explain why, when life challenges engulf us, we can only see the hand of God in it or responsible for it? God is sovereign, and when we declare God's sovereignty over us, we accept the idyllic and the turbulent. Whether it is by our own messes or when darkness covers us, God is with us. With more than a passive presence, God is active with a plan of protection, provision, and empowerment.

God protects. There are times in which only the grace of God kept us from destroying our lives or allowing someone else to destroy us. Remember the occasions in which we made horrendous decisions and played Russian roulette with our lives? Someone fired us from a job or fired us in a relationship, and we ended up on the brink of personal and emotional calamity. Yet there was a keeping quality in God, a God who, as the psalmist says, holds us fast (Psalm 139:10). We were made strong in our weakness.

There is a level of protection that is demonstrated when we are at our wits' end. In the abyss of desolation, we are given a level of stamina to withstand destruction by our spiritual enemy. When the situation would bring others to suicide or murder, God keeps our minds regulated and our hearts fixed on survival. There is an internal resolve to make it. Persons who survived months of abuse, misuse, and neglect and did not die were protected. Persons who survived separation from everything they knew and still lived were protected. We, like they, are being kept and held from losing all hope.

God also provides. God provides a way of existing in and often an escape out of the dungeon. God meets our physical and emotional needs in the dungeon. Our God will not fail. There are some things we cannot do by ourselves. When we look back, it was God's providential nature that provided the slaves food to eat and gave sleep in sleepless nights. They found escape routes, followed a North Star, learned to eat berries off trees, and found water in leaves. Can we look back and remember how we found peace in a financial crisis? Vaseline was a good substitute for the expensive lotions we bought, and living simply did not kill us.

God is leading and guiding us day by day, sometimes moment by moment, painful step after painful step. With God, we must declare "that this destination is not our final location, and this too shall pass." We must fix our compass and change our limitations. When we do, we will know God in ways we did not know God before.

Dungeons will bring either the worst or the best out of us; they will always bring out the best in God. We will either emotionally make it or emotionally dwell in pain and misery. Our setbacks will become comebacks, or will hold us back. It is up to you. Notice that the psalmist David does not say God *may* be with us. David does not say it will be well with us. No, he says, God *is* with us (Psalm 139:7-10).

God empowers. Take that promise, and keep praying and believing. Take those words and get through sickness and pain. God said, "I will be with you." God, who made the heavens and earth, has all power in God's hands. God, who can move in mysterious ways, is with us. God, who knitted us in our mother's womb, is able. God, who made all things, can handle all things.

Ask Daniel and the three Hebrew boys about the dungeon (Daniel 3:19-26; 6:16-23). They know that this same God came down in the fiery furnace, put out the flames, and shut the mouths of lions. This same God kept Mary when pregnant without a husband (Luke 1:26-38) and healed the daughter of the Canaanite woman (Matthew 15:21-28). God allowed Jesus to suffer and to die on the cross, put him in the grave, and then declared that there is no death that does not have some form of resurrection. If you die in the Lord, you will rise again in spirit. If you die in spirit, you will rise again in hope. Our awesome God will do a new thing in you.

Look at us now. Yes, we still have a lot of crime. Yes, we still have a lot of problems. On the other hand, the African diaspora has lawyers, doctors, philosophers, pastors, writers, geneticists, entrepreneurs, educators, entertainers, scientists, sports stars, and healers. We are now working together, building schools in our homelands, bringing clean water through wells, strengthening economies, and healing those with diseases. God has empowered us.

I do not know what the Dutch meant by having that Scripture on the wall. The world may not remember the dungeon, but every time they look at me I will not let them forget. God's Word covers it all and leads us through fire, flame, slavery, drugs, and the valley of death. In some ways they were right; God did ordain it. It was not for their glory or profit but to say to the world, I am in ultimate control, and I will not leave or abandon you.

God does not operate on our time. In our timetable, we see death. In our day, we see affliction and sickness. In our day, we see chaos and despair. But in God's timetable, justice is still on the move, peace is evident, and hope is still abounding. Let us shout the shout of pain until we realize that we can shout the shout of joy. Let's make up our minds to live through it and develop a ministry in the misery. This is the season to have greater compassion for others and appreciate the simplicity of life, the sunset, and rain. Let's work to make sure that no one else has to go through what we have been through. Know God is with us and hear these words from the great hymn:

> In every condition, in sickness, in health;
> In poverty's vale, or abounding in wealth;
> At home and abroad, on the land, on the sea,
> As thy days may demand, shall thy strength ever be.
>
> Fear not, I am with thee, O be not dismayed,
> For I am thy God and will still give thee aid;
> I'll strengthen and help thee, and cause thee to stand
> Upheld by My righteous, omnipotent hand.[3]

A version of this sermon was originally preached at Robinson Community AME Church, Indianapolis, September 1993.

1. eannehenningbyfield, "The Essence of My Existence" (Indianapolis: Masakane Press, 2004), 35.

2. J. Clinton McCann Jr., "The Book of Psalms," *The New Interpreter's Bible,* vol. 4 (Nashville: Abingdon, 1996), 1235.

3. "How Firm a Foundation, Ye Saints of the Lord," Author "K," in John Rippon's *Selection of Hymns, 1787,* tune, early American melody, published in *The African Methodist Episcopal Church Hymnal* (Nashville: African Methodist Episcopal Church, 1984), 433.

9

What's for Dinner?

Carol Antablin Miles

PROVERBS 15:17
Better is a dinner of vegetables where love is than a fatted ox and hatred with it. (Proverbs 15:17, NRSV)

If I had to name one piece of furniture in my parents' home that evokes the strongest memories for me, it would have to be the dining room table. I can still hear the pitch of my mom's voice singing as she'd set down a birthday cake, candles flickering, next to a stack of plates and a tub of ice cream. And I can still sense anticipation as my brother and I turned toward each other on Thanksgiving, each gripping one side of the wishbone, waiting for the signal from my dad to pull. I suppose so many of my memories center on the dinner table because so much of life is shared there. The table is the place where everyday events and activities are narrated, family decisions are negotiated, stories are told, arguments break out, and, at times, tears are shed. You're never quite sure what's going to be served up when a family gathers at the table.

It's no surprise, then, that the sages of Israel, who spent their days observing life in God's created order, had so much to say about life around the dinner table. These teachers of the wisdom school coined proverbs that gave expression to what they had deduced is generally true about the way life works. Long before Stephen Covey came along, the Israelite sages took note of the habits of highly successful people and told their students that it would be wise to do these things, because doing them would more likely than not lead to the good life.

For instance, the book of Proverbs observes, "When you sit down to eat with a ruler, observe carefully what is before you, and put a knife to your throat if you have a big appetite" (23:1, NRSV); "Do not eat the bread of the stingy; do not desire their delicacies; for like a hair in the throat, so are they. 'Eat and drink!' they say to you; but they do not mean it" (23:6-7, NRSV); and finally our text for today, "Better is a dinner of vegetables where love is than a fatted ox and hatred with it."

In this last proverb, the sages remind us of what many couples already know. In the first few days after the 2004 Democratic convention, the press corps following vice presidential candidate John Edwards reported that he and his wife, Elizabeth, stopped along the campaign trail to have dinner at Wendy's. It was their wedding anniversary, they explained, and dinner at Wendy's was their anniversary tradition, dating back to their early years of marriage when money was tight.

I could relate to their story. In the days when my husband and I were young married seminarians, we lived off ramen noodles—prepared in a cast-off pot, eaten on a hand-me-down table. As the years went by and each of us finally got a job, we found our budget could support a real celebration now and then. So, for our wedding anniversary, we splurged and went to dinner at the Four Seasons. Sometime during the salad course, however, one of us brought up a slight that had gone unacknowledged and had been festering under the surface of our life together. When it finally was brought to the surface, the feelings were so raw, the accusations and self-justifications flying back and forth so maddening, that neither of us could eat a bite when the main course was finally served.

"Better is a dinner of vegetables where love is than a fatted ox and hatred with it."

This past summer I rented the film *Pieces of April*.[1] It depicts the story of a nineteen-year-old woman, April, living on the Lower East Side of Manhattan, who volunteers to host Thanksgiving dinner for her family. Her mother, we learn, is in the late stages of breast cancer and enduring chemotherapy. In preparing the meal, April encounters what I consider to be a Thanksgiving host's worst nightmare. After washing and stuffing the bird, she discovers the oven she thought was preheating isn't working. She calls the building superintendent, the city, and the Butterball Turkey Hotline, but finds no one available to help on Thanksgiving. So she begins frantically knocking on doors in

43

her building trying to find anyone willing to let her use their oven as a surrogate. Finally, an African American couple invites her in. She tells them her plight, and they agree to help.

"We'll put off cooking our turkey till 10:30," the wife tells her, "and then you'll have two extra hours to find another oven. How does that sound?" The wife compliments April for doing a meal for her mother and learns April hasn't been home even though her mother is ill. April insists that her mother prefers not to see her.

"I don't believe that."

"It's true. I'm the first pancake."

"The first pancake?"

"The one you're supposed to throw out."

April's assessment of her mother's feelings toward her is not exaggerated. While April is slicing and stirring and stringing crepe paper in the stairwell, we are privy to the conversation her mother and father, sister, brother, and grandmother are having in the car on the way to New York. Convinced the meal will be inedible, her mother leads the others in a mock seminar on "how to discard food from their mouths without their hostess knowing." "Don't get me wrong," her mother volunteers, "I'm glad we're going. This way instead of April showing up with some new piercing or some ugly new tattoo and, God forbid, staying the night, this way we get to show up, experience the disaster that is her life, smile, and go back home."

Meanwhile, April is deflecting praise from the couple who, having convinced her to pitch the can of Ocean Spray, is teaching her how to make homemade cranberry sauce. April becomes increasingly self-conscious about the simplicity of the meal she plans to serve when she hears about the feast her neighbors are making: sweet potato soup, giblet gravy, lemon rosemary green beans, sautéed red Swiss chard with garlic, hickory nut ice cream, and maple pumpkin pie.

In her quest to find a second neighbor willing to offer an oven to finish cooking, April encounters more closed doors, neurotic characters, and one very principled vegan. Finally, Chinese immigrants who speak no English but discern that she's in need of help invite her in. The women of the house take the turkey off her hands, serve her tea, and giggle as she struggles to explain the origins of the Thanksgiving holiday.

April's family eventually arrives in Manhattan, locates her street, and pulls up in front of her apartment. Staring at the overlapping graffiti on the walls of her building, they conclude they were right about April and her irresponsible lifestyle all along, turn the car around, and leave without a word. When April figures out what has happened, she is crushed. But when the door opens on her apartment in the final scene of the movie, she is seated around her modest Thanksgiving table—not with her family, but with her neighbors, those former strangers who had been brought together by an unpredictable turn of events and the sharing of a common meal.

"Better is a dinner of vegetables where love is than a fatted ox and hatred with it."

When we read the Gospels, we discover that Jesus spent a lot of time sitting with people around the dinner table. We're told he often ate with tax collectors and sinners, those whose social status did nothing to advance his own. Once, when he was at the home of Simon the leper, a woman of the city came in, broke open an alabaster jar of costly perfume, anointed Jesus' feet with it, and wet his feet with her tears. Simon grumbled that Jesus couldn't possibly be a prophet or he would have known what kind of woman was touching him. It was then that Jesus told Simon this parable:

> "A certain creditor had two debtors; one owed five hundred denarii, and the other fifty. When they could not pay, he canceled the debts for both of them. Now which of them will love him more?" Simon answered, "I suppose the one for whom he canceled the greater debt."
>
> And Jesus said to him, "You have judged rightly." Then turning toward the woman, he said to Simon, "Do you see this woman? I entered your house; you gave me no water for my feet, but she has bathed my feet with her tears and dried them with her hair. You gave me no kiss, but from the time I came in she has not stopped kissing my feet. You did not anoint my head with oil, but she has anointed my feet with ointment. Therefore, I tell you, her sins, which were many, have been forgiven; hence she has shown great love. But the one to whom little is forgiven, loves little." (Luke 7:41-47, NRSV)

"Better is a dinner of vegetables where love is than a fatted ox and hatred with it."

But why is this proverbial saying true? What have the sages seen that they want to make sure we don't miss? Is it that no one can truly enjoy the good gifts life has to offer if his or her primary relationships are strained? Perhaps. Is it that no amount of feasting and fast living can ultimately satisfy our deepest needs and longings? Maybe. But it seems to me the key to this proverb is found less in focusing on the failure of the fatted ox to satisfy and more in focusing on what happens when one eats and drinks in the presence of love. For, as the writer of 1 John tells us, "Love is from God; everyone who loves is born of God and knows God. Whoever does not love does not know God, for God is love" (4:7-8, NRSV). And according to the Gospel of John, when Jesus gathered his disciples around the table one last time before his crucifixion, he told them, "This is my commandment, that you love one another as I have loved you. No one has greater love than this, to lay down one's life for one's friends" (15:12-13, NRSV).

University Baptist Church, at the center of this house is also a table. And at the heart of this community's life together is a thanksgiving meal. We, who were formerly strangers, have come from our houses, our apartments, our shelters, and our streets and been drawn in close and made into one family, the family of God. And when we gather around this table, Sunday after Sunday, we tell our family story—the story of one who laid down his life for his friends, who gave up his life for the life of the world. For when we gather around this table, we gather in the presence of Love. And there is no greater feast than the feast prepared for us here.

A version of this sermon was preached at University Baptist Church in Austin, Texas, on May 13, 2005.

1. *Pieces of April,* copyright 2003, Well Done Productions, Inc., distributed by MGM Home Entertainment.

10

It Does Get Better

Phyllis Thompson Hilliard

ISAIAH 43:1-4

"When you pass through the waters, I will be with you; and when you pass through the rivers, they will not sweep over you. When you walk through the fire, you will not be burned; the flames will not set you ablaze." (Isaiah 43:2, NIV)

Around 4:30 this morning, God brought a song to my mind that reminded me that when we walk through the waters God will be with us. I sang the song, and I heard the Lord tell me, "You need to tell the people that no matter how ugly it might appear—I'm with you."

I heard somebody say, "No pain, no gain!" Do you think that just goes for exercising? A long time ago when I was complaining, an older Christian woman looked me in the eye, held her finger in my face, and said, "Baby, no cross, no crown!" All through these years, I've done my share of crying and complaining and asking God, "Why? I've done all your Word says to do!" Then I remember that God calls me "precious." I know that anything precious has been tried by fire. It has been crushed. It has been purified, but in the end it looks real good.

Some of the saints here are going through some stuff. Perhaps a handful of us are wondering, *What is going on?* Some of us are facing job losses or have already lost jobs. Some of us are teetering on the brink of foreclosure, and we're trying to find resources to keep the house that God gave us. We've got children asking us, "Why are you crying, Mommy? Mommy, why did they take the car away? How am

I going to get to my football practices?" You're wondering over and again, *What in the name of God is going on?*

I've come to remind us that even in all of this turmoil, it does get better. I've stopped by simply to remind us that God has called us precious. Not only has he called us precious and knows us by name, but the Word of God says we've been honored and God loves us! There is some good news!

When we love somebody, we don't just watch them suffer and wait to see how long it's going to be before they cry uncle. We go out and rescue them—we assist them. We may be saying, "God, your Word declares that I'm precious in your sight, but I'm standing here in a situation where it seems I'm never going to get relief. I have no more recourse. I have no more resources! God, I need a breakthrough! I need you to answer my cry and answer my prayer."

Jesus said that "in this world you will have trouble." He went on to say, "But take heart! I have overcome the world" (John 16:33, NIV). Yes, you had the car repossessed, but I drive by car lots all the time, and they're full of vehicles. And I've been acquainted with God long enough to know that God is a God of miracles. This won't be for long! It will get better!

I'm not talking about magic. Lamentations 3:23 says that God's mercies "are new every morning; great is [God's] faithfulness." So if God is faithful, then this suggests that it will not be much longer before there is a turning of the tide. Hold on to your faith! Don't begin to doubt God. Don't use some illegal means to get some extra money! No, my brother and my sister! Trust God, who has honored you and declared that he loves you. It will get better.

The other day, a sister shared with my husband that she felt as if she were drowning. I began to resonate with that sister, because I have had situations that felt like they were clogging up my nostrils, that the water was way past my eyeballs—couldn't see, couldn't breathe, couldn't cry for help. But, oh, help did come! God is not going to stand by and see one of his children in distress and do nothing. Just when you give up and think, *This is it*—someone comes along and scoops you up, high above the waters you thought were going to take you under. Only God; only God!

Bishop [Hilliard] shared last Thursday that some of us may very well have to downsize. We may have to learn to live on less, and we may have to change our way of living. We've become accustomed to having so much. God is faithful—even in the downsizing. If you have to forfeit the custom-made house to move into an apartment—this is still the will of God in Christ Jesus concerning you. You still have a place to call home. You still have a roof over your head. You still have peace of mind. You still have yourself intact. You are still loved by God.

A few weeks ago I was watching, as many of you did, Spike Lee's documentary film highlighting the aftermath of Hurricane Katrina.[1] He interviewed and recorded many of the displaced residents and the conditions of that great city. My attention was particularly drawn to one woman, Phyllis. She, like most, had been uprooted and lost everything. At one point during her interview, she said she had thought about suicide. "But I thought about it, and I realized that I have a lot to live for."[2] I sat there in the comfort of my family room, and I said, "There you go, girl! You sure do; I agree!" Her situation was beyond devastating. Can you imagine walking around a place where your house used to be and now there's nothing; it's completely leveled?

We're complaining about high gas prices; here was someone whose car ended up in another state! This is someone whose home has been reduced to rubble, but she was able to say, "I have something to live for." That taught me volumes! Phyllis didn't mention God right away; as a matter of fact, she cussed a few times. She never mentioned salvation. She didn't give a sprawling testimony. This woman simply said, in essence, "I came to myself; I have a reason to live." Later, when she showed off her new trailer, Phyllis said, "It ain't like home, but I thank God it's someplace for me to lay my head." Again, I felt the Lord tap me on the shoulder and say, "The little bit that she has, without really expressing that she knows me, she's got enough presence of mind—enough good sense to give me thanks, to acknowledge that it will get better."

I've been playing phone tag with Wachovia Bank myself. They're threatening to take my dead momma's house. I tell you, I have never written so many letters and made so many phone calls. But I told them if they'd just give me a chance—hold on—no padlocks—no sheriff's sale—just hold on. This morning my daughter brought me the mail from my mother's house, and there was a check in there. So I'll be making my way to the bank to say, "This represents the two months that you've been badgering me about."

I'm determined not to lose my peace. When I put the phone down after talking to the bank representative, I went on doing what I was doing. Then, I thought for a moment, *Phyllis, do you understand? The woman said "foreclosure."* I unfolded the letter and read it again: great big print—"NOTICE OF FORECLOSURE." I realized I really didn't have it—but God does. Through the years, I've gotten bold enough to make some demands on God. I reminded him that his Word says he owns the cattle on a thousand hills (Psalm 50:10). Right now, I don't need any cattle. But if you could exchange that for some cash, Lord, this sister would be all right!

Let's remind ourselves again and again that through it all, up and down, in and out, advance and reverse—it does get better. All thy battles, I will fight, the songwriter says about God. We will not be consumed! We will not go under! We are not going to lose our minds! Go ahead and try to have a nervous breakdown—I dare you! It does get better! Thanks be to God!

A version of this sermon was preached at The Cathedral International, Perth Amboy, New Jersey, on October 8, 2006.

1. *When the Levees Broke,* directed by Spike Lee, HBO Television, March 2007.
2. Ibid.

11

Called to Be a Dabar People

Elizabeth Conde-Frazier

ISAIAH 60:1-3

"Arise, shine, for your light has come, and the glory of the LORD rises upon you." (Isaiah 60:1, NIV)

Isaiah 60 tells us there is darkness over the earth. What is this darkness? Isaiah describes it as darkness and gloom so thick we stumble at noon as at twilight. What is this darkness? It is injustice! Injustice is when God's love is flowing to all but a few decide to hoard it for themselves—God bless me and nobody else. They dam up God's love so that it seems to become absent from the lives of others—the poor, the immigrant, the abused, the exploited, those without health care, those abandoned to HIV/AIDS.

The global economy has indulged our sensibilities such that we have become predators and prey. Asian theologian C. S. Song says that as economic globalization goes on by leaps and bounds, the earth has become a theater in which people eat people: the rich eat the poor; the powerful eat the powerless; oppressors eat the oppressed; and the developed eat the underdeveloped.[1] Advertising has taught us that our desires are our needs, and we have lost the ability to discern between the two.

What is light in the midst of such darkness? What does justice look like? In the United States, before the civil rights movement, churches spoke of love but could not articulate what that love looked like. During the movement, Dr. Martin Luther King Jr. equated justice with love. He said, "Justice is love correcting that which would work against love."[2] Who will do this in the name of the Lord? It will be the children of light. Is the ABC family these children of light? Think before you answer. The web of injustice is so tightly woven that it takes great creativity and persistence to unravel it. It takes the spirituality of resistance and solidarity.

In solidarity we enter the agony of hopelessness and powerlessness. Some of us turn off the news when we see this agony, but children of light enter into it. Solidarity enters into the pain of a future denied to the poor and millions of immigrants worldwide displaced by the global economy. Solidarity is the torment of seeing potential harvests of hope eaten up by a worm, leaving only futility and despair. It is responding with more creative ways to plant and to believe that you will yet see a harvest. Are we children of light?

In Matthew 5:14-16, the metaphor of light presents disciples as illumination for the world. The metaphor of the city on a hill presents the disciples as inevitably and unavoidably being seen. There is a tension in the book of Matthew, because in Matthew 6 others should not see your good works—"do not let your left hand know what your right hand is doing" (NIV). Yet here, others are to see our light. How do we deal with this tension?

In Dostoyevsky's novel *The Brothers Karamazov*, Father Zosima, a wise and holy monk, has a conversation with a distraught woman who says she has a problem that is destroying her. She explains that at some point in her life—she doesn't know why, because there was no great crisis in her life—she ceased to believe in God. It happened slowly, bit by bit, until now she is shocked to realize that she no longer believes. Now everything is tasteless and colorless to her; it has all turned to ashes. Zosima tells her that she must go home and every day, without fail, in the most concrete and practical way possible, love the people around her.

You see, the only workable proof for the existence of God is an experience of daily, concrete love for those around us. Long ago we were told by the author of the first letter of John that anyone claiming to love God, whom he cannot see, while not loving the sister whom he can see, is a liar. One cannot know *who* God is, and therefore *that* God is (i.e., that God exists) if one never knows agape love.

But we are claiming to know God and to have an experience of God. In the "seek it" interviews that we carried out in Green Lake, one person explained that at his brother's funeral—the only time he'd ever been to a church—he saw the personal care and compassion of the people in the church around the period of mourning and comfort, and suddenly he was able to understand what the eulogist was talking about. He felt those words about God connect deeply to his life. Can you see the connection between love and the understanding that God exists? Our call to discipleship is the call to self-giving love. Jesus' ultimate service is the gift of his life in love. We are called to love as Jesus loved; this love is our servanthood.

Believers are called to follow Jesus to his death but also are offered the promise of sharing in Jesus' glorification. In other words, we die to our life for love of those whom God loves and for whom Jesus died; then we are honored by God. It is when a believing community is honored by God that it shines! It shines not to show off but because we can't help but shine. God is shining from within us.

"Arise and shine" means that first we must lay on the altar all our self-made ambitions and dreams in order to receive God's dreams, God's will, the desires of God's heart. And what does God desire in today's world? To heal its brokenness, to reconcile, to bring salvation or health or well-being or wholeness. God desires shalom. God desires the release of darkness for prisoners, preaching good news to the poor, which means jobs and dignity and shelter. What is the desire of God's heart? That we act justly, that we love mercy—that we become compassionate. If we want to see miracles, act in compassion. Setting ourselves apart for this type of deep, steady affection is our spiritual worship.

Radical discipleship is about fixing our eyes upon Jesus. For Latinos, to see Jesus on the cross is to see our brothers and sisters who suffer. For American Baptist missionary Lauran Bethell, it is to see young women who are used for human trafficking and to see a child of God who needs to be released into a future of hope. For Martin Luther King Jr., it was to see people denied their basic human rights and to see God's dream of equality and dignity. At first King saw his own people, but as he grew in his gaze upon Jesus, the people he saw became all poor and broken peoples, even those whom his own nation considered enemies. To fix our eyes upon our suffering Lord is to claim for ourselves the privilege of the cross. What is this privilege? To be broken, to feel anger because we can see injustices; and we have to make others aware of these as well. It is to accept the priesthood of all believers. We all minister as a community of light. What is the privilege of the cross? It is the privilege of losses, it is grief and tears because we do feel compassion, and from this compassion flows imagination, healing; resurrection power is released. Do not pray to be delivered from these pangs, but rejoice. Rejoice because those who suffer with Christ are likewise glorified with him.

Glorification, my brothers and sisters, is a mark. We are branded with the sign of the cross. From our radical discipleship comes our blessing where God exalts us—honors us, glorifies us; and in this glorification comes our shining. We are decorated in a display of light that spreads a finer joy, a great brightness and luster. We become radiant. We are sent off as rays from the source of light. Jesus is the light of the world, and those who spend time in his presence, eyes fixed upon him, are sent off as rays of brightness of love to the brokenness of the world. Their riches or gifts of the spirit make a splendid appearance as works of mercy and healing, and they display a brilliant glory. Yes, your light will shine from the hill of Golgotha, from the hill of your city, of your town. Arise and shine!

People who shine are a Pentecost people, for Pentecost was not about individual gifts. Pentecost is a revolution, the explosion of love among us and through us and released and poured out into the world to redeem, to regain and reclaim life from the clutches of death—to bring light into darkness. Let us arise and shine! Let us preach an incarnated Word. In a time of many words, counterfeit words, only an incarnated Word will feed the great spiritual hunger of this generation that cries out for authentic community. *Dabar* is a Hebrew word that means word as event. In an oral culture, words are not on a flat surface, but they have power over things. Our words have the power to bless and to curse, and as soon as they are spoken, they become an action taking place or about to take place among us. Word as event is when my words become deeds and my deeds become an expression of servanthood. This servanthood gives forth fruit. This fruit may be an alteration, however slight, in our world. But these variances accumulate until there is a noticeable difference that we can capture a semblance of the kingdom, the basileia of God.

Dabar requires integrity, the coordination of our ideals and our practices—our vision statements and actions that make a difference. Our thoughts must become actions; our actions must become habits because our habits become character, and the momentum of all of these working together become the power that determines the course of events in our congregations—it determines whether we are to be healthy churches. Healthy churches have a vision of the cross of Jesus, of the expression of their radical discipleship in the community. Healthy churches are conformed unto the pattern of Jesus' death and transformed into the power of his resurrection. When a church becomes healthy, there is no time for agendas under the table; there is only time for ministry.

American Baptists, people of radical discipleship, people committed to actions that make a difference—arise and shine. We are beginning a new century in our history. What shall our witness be? Baptists in the fifteenth and sixteenth centuries were known as a baptizing church; in the seventeenth century, we were known as an obedient church; in the eighteenth century, as a free church; in the nineteenth century Baptists were an apostolic church.[3] In the last century, we were a righteous church. But in this century, we must be known as a *dabar* church, a people of the incarnated Word. We must not only preach the gospel; we must be the gospel, and so be children of light.

Arise and shine! See the pain of the world through the eyes of our Lord. Weep for the people Jesus loves and died for, and let the Spirit carve out a deep place in us where God pours agape love. Arise, don't leave here the same. Let us place our dreams, our ambitions, our agendas, and our whole life before God here and now. This is a life-changing moment. Let the Spirit do in us what needs to be done to heal our church and make it righteous. Let's allow Christ to mark us as people of the cross, as his disciples, as children of light. Let Jesus pour into us power to embrace the world as neighbor. Let us allow the Spirit to energize us for servant ministries of evangelism, social justice, peacemaking, new church development, and economic development and education. Let us be convicted, commissioned, and committed. Let us leave here a faithful people, children of light, a *dabar* people for a new century. Arise and shine! Hallelujah! Arise and shine!

A version of this sermon was preached at the biennial centennial celebration of the American Baptist Churches Sunday worship service on July 1, 2007, at the Washington Convention Center, Washington, D.C.

1. C. S. Song, *And Their Eyes Are Opened: Story Sermons Embracing the World* (St. Louis, MO: Chalice Press, 2006), 65.

2. Martin Luther King Jr., "Address to the Initial Mass Meeting of the Montgomery Improvement Association," at the Hold Street Baptist Church, December 5, 1955. The tape and printed copy of this address are located in the Martin Luther King Jr. Papers, Center for Non-Violent Social Change, Atlanta.

3. See Curtis W. Freeman, James Wm. McClendon Jr., and C. Rosalee Velloso Ewell, *Baptist Roots: A Reader in the Theology of a Christian People* (Valley Forge, PA: Judson Press, 1999).

12

A Cracked Cistern, a Living God

Donna E. Allen

JEREMIAH 2:1-19

"For my people have committed two evils: they have forsaken me, the fountain of living water, and dug out cisterns for themselves, cracked cisterns that can hold no water." (Jeremiah 2:13, NRSV).

The book of Jeremiah begins with a proper prophetic introduction, the call narrative. The call narrative identifies the prophet's mission: plucking up and pulling down, destroying and overthrowing (Jeremiah 1:10). The call narrative identifies the prophet's commissioner, God. Jeremiah tries to resist the irresistible call by God to the terrible task of speaking truth to power. Jeremiah knows he will be rejected by the people, both prophet and prophecy. Jeremiah complains, but it is clear the living God has called Jeremiah.

Jeremiah's qualms of inadequacy are irrelevant; the issue is not what Jeremiah can or cannot do but that his activity is under the initiative of God. As a prophet, Jeremiah is sent to say "thus says the LORD." That is what prophets in ancient Israel were—messengers and mouthpieces for God. Unfortunately for Jeremiah, the message from God was a message of judgment upon the people of God called Judah. We can identify with Jeremiah's quandary, for nobody really wants to be the bearer of bad news. So we understand Jeremiah's resistance. But God rejects Jeremiah's objection. Has anybody had God reject your objection to being used by God? You tell God, "I'm too young, I'm too old, I'm a woman, I can't talk in front of people, I don't speak English, I'm gay, I'm bisexual, I'm divorced, nobody is going to listen to me," and God stamps your objection "REJECTED", tells you that you are chosen, and directs you to move forward in faith remembering that you, too, have been created in the image of God.

Jeremiah's prophetic activity covered a tumultuous period of Judah's history. It swayed from some high times during the reign of King Josiah, who sought to reform the religious life of the nation, and plummeted to low times, the fall of Jerusalem and Judah, the exile of many in Judah to Babylon, and even Jeremiah's exile to Egypt. The ministry of Jeremiah begins in a time of glory and ends in a time of judgment. Jeremiah proclaimed Judah's downfall as the judgment of God, which is why Jeremiah is known as a prophet of doom. Oracle after oracle, word after word, Jeremiah calls the people to repent, to amend their ways, to amend the sin in their worship, in their social life, and in their relationships with one another. But Judah rejects the prophet Jeremiah. Judah rejects the poetic oracles. Judah rejects God.

At the heart of Jeremiah 2 is an image of a courtroom scene. Foreign nations from the coasts of Cyprus to the inlands of Kedar are gathered to hear a covenant lawsuit. All creation presses near to listen as the plaintiff, God, brings a case against the defendant, Judah. The charge is faithlessness. The opening statement of God begins with a historical glance. Judah is told to remember. Remember the early days of your relationship with God. Remember your youth. Remember your initial devotion to God. O, how you loved God. Remember? Remember when we first joined the church. Remember when we thought all parishioners were pious, pleasant people. Some of us wore big crosses, carried big black Bibles with our names etched in gold letters. Remember? Remember how you loved God. Every other word from our mouths was "Praise the Lord." Remember?

The first word of the Lord through Jeremiah is a powerful, poignant recollection of Judah's youthful love and devotion. Remember the triumph over Pharaoh in the exodus experience. Remember the trials and victories in the wilderness all the way to the covenantal moment at Sinai. The point of the divine request to recollect is not to identify an idyllic time like the good old days, but rather to remember a relationship with God as it was and is still meant to be: the people put their trust and security in the God of their deliverance. As Judah remembers with fondness, the prophet interrupts their nostalgia and bellows, "Thus says the Lord, the memory of Israel's devotion is precisely that, a memory, a recollection from the past!" For the present is another story. The people have left God and gone after worthless things, gone after idols. They have given loyalty and devotion due only to the living God to idols. In God is to be found the source of life and security. Seeking this elsewhere is an utterly fruitless task. It is, the prophet says, like "broken cisterns." The people of God have forsaken God, the "fountain of living waters," for broken cisterns.

Let me put the analogy in context. In the setting of the text, the land is very dry. Water is in short supply. Water is so scarce you can't even break a sweat. To combat the lack of water, the people built cisterns, large clay vessels strategically shaped to capture rainwater and surface runoff water. The lower part of these often pear-shaped cisterns was placed underground so the water captured would not evaporate. The cisterns were placed anywhere possible, as many as possible. Imagine you are thirsty, the sun stings your skin, whirling sand dust coats your throat, and your eyes burn red with thirst. The sight of a cistern gives a glimmer of hope for relief. When you get to the cistern, you discover it is cracked and there is no water; the water has seeped out, escaped to the ground. In the text, Jeremiah declares the people have committed evil against God: "They have forsaken [God], the fountain of living water, and dug out cisterns for themselves, cracked cisterns that can hold no water" (2:13, NRSV). Judah has abandoned God for other gods, and they are worthless, worthless like a cracked cistern.

It is difficult in our contemporary context to imagine that we could abandon God as Judah did. We can't imagine shifting our loyalty to God to worthless things. Idolatry is a somewhat antiquated theological concept for modern, indeed postmodern minds, to comprehend. Idolatry—it even sounds ancient. Idolatry is placing one's hope or security in anything or anyone other than God. Perhaps idolatry begins as a subtle shift in trust. We don't build an altar to a foreign god, but rather we begin to look for life-changing events like winning the lottery that will set us free from financial shortfalls. We daydream about what we will do with the winnings, including paying our tithes; we imagine even hope for such good fortune. This is a subtle shift in our faith that gives way to a shift in our loyalty and invites a shift in our security and worship. All are idolatry. Perhaps modern prophets

59

need particularly be mindful of idolatry, for we are susceptible to seek the worth of our witness in the praises of people. Jeremiah reminds us that our worth as God's mouthpiece is not determined by the response of the people but by our obedience to God. Success in our ministries is not based on the head count of congregations, big budgets, or the size of buildings, but rather on obedience to God. In our culture, we have a pantheon of places where we seek security and meaning: money, immediate gratification, military strength, pleasure, hero worship, self-worship. All cracked cisterns, all worthless.

We can resist cistern-mentality idolatry by remembering; remembering how we got over, remembering the God of our deliverance who has brought us a long way. Remember how we met God at the cross, the mystery of God made known to us; remember our call to ministry, that irresistible invitation to serve in spite of feelings of inadequacy that are slowly erased in the realization of our total dependence on the living God. We can resist a cistern mentality every time we remember the power of the living God who has called us to speak truth to power. Remember we are not our own, but rather we have been bought with a price. Remember, and be faithful to the fountain of living water, our God whose life flows through us and into the world.

This sermon was prepared as a classroom illustration for the author's homiletics students at Lancaster Theological Seminary in Lancaster, Pennsylvania.

13

Managing Life's Challenges

Carla Jean-McNeil Jackson

HABAKKUK 3:16-19

I hear, and my body trembles, my lips quiver at the sound; rottenness enters into my bones, my steps totter beneath me. I will quietly wait for the day of trouble to come upon people who invade us. Though the fig tree do not blossom, nor fruit be on the vines, the produce of the olive fail and the fields yield no food, the flock be cut off from the fold and there be no herd in the stalls ... (Habakkuk 3:16-17, RSV)

In 2007, ABC aired "Building a Dream: The Oprah Winfrey Leadership Academy,"[1] which chronicles the inception of Oprah Winfrey's boarding school for girls in South Africa. In this one-hour special, many of the girls say in their own words how things have been hard, yet they are able to achieve amid adversity. Thando, age thirteen, reared by her grandmother, wants to be South Africa's first female president. Living with her grandparents because her mother died from AIDS, twelve-year-old Zodwa is afraid when she comes home from school because "people carry guns, knives" and "boys are grabbing you." Nevertheless, she walks that road to school every day because she wants to be "a leader" and "an example." At ages five and six, Sade and Megan were orphaned because, in the midst of an argument, their father shot their mother and then shot himself. But despite their horror, Oprah describes Sade as "walking sunshine" and wonders, with their dim history, "Where does that light come from?"[2] It is the story of the brilliance of all of these girls that led me to the book of Habakkuk.

The prophet Habakkuk lived under rising Babylonian power. It was a time of brutality and bloodshed, as King Nebuchadnezzar quickly and without hindrance moved through Habakkuk's homeland to Egypt and destroyed the Egyptian army, which previously controlled Palestine and parts of Syria. So, in chapter 1, Habakkuk challenges God who sees but does not intervene. YHWH says things will get worse before they get better. The situation is dramatic. There is conflict, violence, injustice, idolatry, famine, and illness. Yet, in these tough times, Habakkuk writes a song of hope.

But unlike Habakkuk and the girls from South Africa who vow to keep going in the midst of their tragedy, we do not always remain productive when we face hard times. We do things we should not do because we are unable to cope with our circumstances. Consequently, we are prone to plunge into a period of detrimental living. We spiral into destructive behaviors by overeating when we feel stressed. We harass an old flame by constantly calling because we refuse to accept the relationship is over. Or we max out our credit cards through our compulsive shopping for a temporary sense of relief. If we continue to harm ourselves, we will become broken. If we become broken, we will lose self-esteem. If we lose self-esteem, we will not see our true value. If we do not see our true value, we will lose our sense of purpose. As in Habakkuk's day, we will be like the fig tree that has no blossom.

The first step to managing life's challenges is admitting our reality. We must candidly confront our crisis and see our situation as it is. It is imperative that we face the facts, since acceptance is the first step to recovery. We can tell the truth by taking inventory of our situation or crying on a friend's shoulder. Or, like Habakkuk in verses 16 and 17, we can tell God about our trouble.

In our text, verses 16 and 17, Habakkuk confesses his concerns to God in a psalm. The fig trees have no blossoms, and there are no grapes on the vine. The fig tree symbolizes prosperity and peace, and the fig also is used as a laxative and a cure for swelling. Both figs and grapes are used to make wine. So, not only is Habakkuk living in a time of poverty and conflict, but also there is no medicine to cure disease and no wine to dull the pain. Additionally, the failed olive crop sabotages the society's success because the olive is necessary for cooking, lighting, and ointments. Moreover, the fields and the cattle barns are empty. Thus, in addition to the violence in chapter 1, chapter 3 details deprived conditions with no cattle or crops for nourishment, medicine, or trade.

Rather than piously ignore the situation, Habakkuk admits that things are not going well. And like the prophet, we should admit what is going on in our lives. If we are hungry, we need someone to feed us or buy our groceries. If we have been evicted, we need someone to open up his or her door to us. If we are sick, we need someone to pledge with the Tom Joyner crew to "Take a Loved One to the Doctor."[3] It is time to engage in what renowned feminist bell hooks calls "truth telling."[4] The Eternal does not expect us to be sightless about our situation. If we deny our problems, we will be less apt to find ways to fix them. But like Habakkuk and the girls from South Africa, we cannot allow difficulty to lead us to despair.

After we admit our reality, the second step to managing life's challenges is to adjust our attitude. The Almighty has come to our aid. We can, in the words of Jesse Jackson, "keep hope alive" because the Lord has a history of lifting people up. We can, as the song goes, count our many blessings and "name them one by one,"[5] or read old journal entries to remind us when we got through other life events. Or, akin to Habakkuk in verse 18, we can transition out of our sadness with a "yet."

Habakkuk does not deny the evil he faces, but he does not surrender to it either. He acknowledges the problems, and then in verse 18 says, "Yet I will rejoice in the LORD, I will joy in the God of my salvation." Habakkuk could adjust his attitude from complaint to celebration because God has saved before. In verse 2 of this chapter, the Good News translation reads, "O LORD, I have heard of what you have done, and I am filled with awe." Though Habakkuk is frustrated, he changes his perception when he considers God's reputation. With God, people have survived trouble and managed challenges before. We do not have to be discouraged. Instead, we can follow Habakkuk's example and think back. If God worked it out before, God can do it again.

After we admit our reality and adjust our attitude, the last step to managing life's challenges is to acknowledge the source of our strength. The Most High can give us the muscle to climb mountains. We must cooperate with the Architect of our lives. Cultivating a relationship is the key. We gain power by partnering with El Shaddai, who grants us strength to tread upon heights. We partner by asking for direction through prayer, allowing God to order our steps.

Habakkuk's problems are overwhelming but not insurmountable. He says in verse 19, "God, the Lord, is my strength; he makes my feet like hinds' feet, he makes me tread upon my high places" (RSV). The prophet is confident that, like deer, he will hold well on the roads of life with help from the Divine. We may not have power to move mountains, but we can keep going. Our Maker will give us strong, deerlike legs. With God, we can finish our degree and become our own boss. With God, we can get a recording contract and beat an illness. With God, we can finish our book and recover from bad relationships.

When we acknowledge the source of our strength, we follow the forerunner of our faith, Jesus. Just as Jesus was betrayed, we will bear some burdens. Just as Jesus was hung high, we will have some hard knocks. And just as Jesus was crucified, we will contend with catastrophe. And, just as Jesus denied death, we can defy defeat. As Jesus was resurrected, we can recover from ruin. Like Jesus, we can triumph over tragedy and glory after grief. Like Jesus, we can succeed in a struggle, achieve amid adversity, and conquer any crisis.

In the end, we can confront life's challenges and, following the instructions in verse 19, sing a song of hope. "I've got a feeling everything's gonna be all right."[6]

Versions of this sermon were preached at St. Paul's Baptist Church in Richmond, Virginia, September 17, 2006, and at Jerusalem Baptist Church in Sparta, Virginia on March 4, 2007.

1. American Broadcasting Company, "Building a Dream: The Oprah Winfrey Leadership Academy," aired February 26, 2007.

2. "Meet the Girls," http://www.oprah.com/presents/2007/academy/girls/girls_main.jhtml (accessed July 24, 2007).

3. The third Tuesday of September is "Take a Loved One to the Doctor Day," a health initiative sponsored by Tom Joyner and others to encourage people of

color to receive medical attention. See "Operation Healthy U.S., Part One: 'Take a Loved One to the Doctor' Day," BlackAmericaWeb.com; http://www.black americaweb.com/site.aspx/bawnews/ealthyuspt1913 (accessed August 28, 2007).

4. See bell hooks, *Sisters of the Yam: Black Women and Self-Recovery* (Cambridge: South End Press, 1993).

5. Johnson Oatman Jr. and Edwin O. Excell, "Count Your Blessings," 1897.

6. Olanda Draper, author and composer, "Gotta Feelin'," on the album *Gotta Feelin'*, Olanda Draper & Associates, Warner Bros., 1996.

New Testament
SERMONS

14

Good News for the Jews

Wil Gafney

MATTHEW 9:35–10:15
Then Jesus went about all the cities and villages, teaching in their synagogues, and proclaiming the good news of the kingdom, and curing every disease and every sickness. (Matthew 9:35, NRSV)

On this Young Adult Sunday, we are reminded that all of us are called to be disciples. It doesn't matter how old or young we are, feel, or think we are. As we saw on the dance floor at the Young Adult cabaret, youth is a mental construct within some physical parameters. Today's Gospel includes a story about the first twelve disciples, but they were not the only disciples. There were many others in their generation and in the generations that followed; we are their descendants.

> After healing many, Yeshua [in his own language, Jesus in ours] went around all the cities and villages in the Galil, teaching in their synagogues, and proclaiming the good news of the reign of God, and curing every disease and every sickness. When he saw the crowds, he had compassion for them, because they were harassed and helpless, like sheep without a shepherd.

After healing many Judeans, Jews, Yeshua, Jesus, went about all the Judean, Jewish, cities and villages in the Galil, teaching in their synagogues, proclaiming the good news of the reign of God, and curing every disease and every sickness. When he saw the crowds of

69

Jewish people, he had compassion for them, because they were harassed and helpless, like sheep without a shepherd. At this point, the ministry and mission of Yeshua, Jesus, the Jewish messiah, is only to the Jewish people.

Yeshua, Jesus, sent out the twelve apostles with the following instructions: "Do not go any way leading to Gentiles, and do not enter any Samaritan town, but go rather to the lost sheep of the house of Israel. As you go rather to the lost sheep of the house of Israel, proclaim, 'The reign of heaven has come near.' Cure the sick in the house of Israel, raise the dead in the house of Israel, cleanse the lepers in the house of Israel, and cast out demons in the house of Israel." This is good news for Jews, but what about the rest of us?

This Gospel is exclusive, and we who were not born Jewish are not included in today's lesson. In fact, Yeshua prohibited the apostles from preaching to anyone who was not Jewish. They were even prohibited from preaching to those who shared some Jewish ancestry, the Samaritans. The Jewish messiah sounds uncomfortably ethnocentric; not at all like the Jesus we know and love as our own personal savior.

Why would the Messiah have a bias against Gentiles? We need to remember that part of the mystery of the incarnation is the fusion of humanity and divinity. The church has sometimes failed to emphasize the humanity of Christ. But he was as much human as he was divine, and in this text he has some very human cultural assumptions and baggage. And he came by them honestly. For as far back as anyone could remember, Israel always had a rocky relationship with Gentile nations. The Egyptians enslaved them; then there were all of those fights with the *-ites*—Canaanites, Jebusites, Hittites, Hivites, Perizzites, Amorites. Next, the Assyrians occupied them; the Babylonians invaded them and destroyed their temple; the Persians conquered them; the Greeks assimilated them; and the Romans oppressed them. The Gentile-Jewish distinction is another way of saying, "It's us versus them." And from the point of view of any first-century Jew, "they" were bad news to "us." And we Gentiles are them, not us, outsiders, not insiders.

But what about the Samaritans? They were Jewish too. Yes, but they were regarded as insincere converts. When Samaria was Israel's capital, the Assyrians attacked and carried away everyone who someone thought was important. The Assyrians transplanted people from Babylon, Cuthah, Avva, Hamath, and Sepharvaim who married what was left of the Samaritans. They had so many different religious practices that a priest was sent from Beth-El to teach them how to worship the God of Israel. Their descendants became known as the Samaritans. The Judean neighbors thought of them as leftover, half-breed converts. Against that background, hear the words of the Gospel again: "Yeshua, Jesus, sent out the Twelve with the following instructions: Do not go any way leading to Gentiles, and do not enter any Samaritan town, but go rather to the lost sheep of the house of Israel."

I know he's the Son of God, but he seems to have a cultural bias against most of God's children. The Gentiles are everyone who was not born Jewish; the Samaritans were at least born Jewish but not counted as Jewish enough. Suddenly that doesn't sound like good news for you and me. But in chapter 15 of this same Gospel, Yeshua, Jesus, has an experience that changes him forever. Most folks think that as human and divine, Jesus came into this world knowing everything. I want to suggest that part of his being human was learning and growing, so that his experience of humanity would be authentic. I believe that one of his most transformational experiences was a conversation with a Gentile woman:

> Yeshua, Jesus, left Gennesaret and went away to the district of Tyre and Sidon. Just then a Canaanite woman from that region came out and started shouting, "Have mercy on me, Lord, Son of David; my daughter is tormented by a demon." But he did not answer her at all. And his disciples came and urged him, saying, "Send her away, for she keeps shouting after us." He answered, "I was sent only to the lost sheep of the house of Israel." But she came and knelt before him, saying, "Lord, help me." He answered, "It is not fair to take the children's food and throw it to the dogs." She said, "Yes, Lord, yet even the dogs eat the crumbs that fall from their masters' table." Then Yeshua, Jesus, answered her, "Woman, great is your faith! Let it be done for you as you wish." And her daughter was healed instantly. (Matthew 15:21-28)

This woman received not only grace and healing for her daughter, but she paved the way for all of us who were not of the house of Israel to receive the gospel.

The closing words of this Gospel teach us that Christ has made room at the table for everyone, Jew and Gentile alike: "Go therefore and make disciples of all nations, baptizing them in the name of the

Father and of the Son and of the Holy Spirit, and teaching them to obey everything that I have commanded you. And remember, I am with you always, to the end of the age" (Matthew 28:18-20, NRSV).

Last week, Father Shaw reminded us that it is nothing less than grace that the Jewish messiah would come to redeem the whole world, Gentiles included. None of us has a right to the Tree of Life or even the Lord's Supper.

Even after Jesus threw the doors of the church wide open to admit "whosoever" would take refuge in the ark of safety—male, female, Jew, Gentile, slave, free, gay, straight, crooked—Gentile-Jewish relations remained a problem for the early church. The fathers of the church argued about which commandments from the Hebrew Scriptures were binding on Gentile Christians. In just a few years, Gentiles would become so dominant that they began to forget that they were graciously adopted into the house of Israel.

In Romans 11, the apostle Paul, originally named Sha'ul, who was himself a Pharisee of the tribe of Benjamin, reminded his Gentile converts that they were grafted into the "rich root of the olive tree," the Israelite faith. He reminded them that the grace they received was still extended to that original branch.

In spite of God's grace, cultural bias has lurked behind the pages of the Gospel since the days of the Messiah. The church has moved from one ethnic hegemony to another. One of the great sorrows of Christian history is that we have turned our backs on our Jewish brothers and sisters in such a way as to permit the decimation of the house of Israel in the Shoah, the Holocaust. Professor Johanna Bos puts it more directly: The Holocaust was "perpetrated in Christian lands by baptized hands."[1]

When we focus on what divides us, we forget what unites us, like being made in the image of God. On close examination, the us-them binary falls apart. After all, Abraham, the father of Jewish people was neither Jewish nor even Israelite. He was from Chaldea, what would become Babylon and later Iraq. Joseph opened the door to the enslavement of his own people in Egypt by setting up a system in which those who didn't have enough money to buy grain during the famine could sell themselves. Joseph married an Egyptian woman, Asenath. The Israelites left Egypt with a mixed multitude of folks from different nations that led to many more interethnic marriages.

Moses apparently never found an Israelite woman he liked, because he married a Midianite woman and later left her for a Nubian sister. And of course Ruth, the grandmother of King David, was a Moabite; these non-Israelites did not have the right to enter the presence of the Holy One of Sinai.

I have an icon of the blessed Virgin Mary with the Christ Child still in her womb. He is holding a Torah scroll and wearing a *tallit*, a traditional Jewish prayer shawl. She is wearing a Nazi yellow Star of David and is surrounded by barbed wire. That icon reminds me that there can be no us without them.

The gospel is that Jesus Christ has torn down every wall of separations that separates humanity from divinity and divides humanity against itself. There is no longer Jew or Greek, there is no longer slave or free, there is no longer male and female, for we are all one in Christ Jesus (Galatians 3:28). Amen!

A version of this sermon was originally delivered on June 5, 2005, at the African Episcopal Church of St. Thomas, Philadelphia. Dr. Gafney teaches Hebrew and provides the translation for all texts, including the Greek texts, when she preaches.

1. Johanna Bos is Dora Pierce Professor of Bible and professor of Old Testament at Louisville Presbyterian Theological Seminary, the first woman to be tenured at the school. She grew up in Holland under Nazi occupation and witnessed the treatment of Jews.

15

Shimoni

Emily C. Hassler

MARK 12:38-44

A poor widow came and put in two small copper coins, which are worth a penny. Then he called his disciples and said to them, "Truly I tell you, this poor widow has put in more than all those who are contributing to the treasury. For all of them have contributed out of their abundance; but she out of her poverty has put in everything she had, all she had to live on." (Mark 12:42-44, NRSV)

My name is Shimoni; it means "she who hears," and I did hear him that day in the temple courtyard. As a child, my parents were fond of suggesting that I could hear a conversation taking place three houses away. My father was always concerned that I would get myself into trouble listening where I should not, especially at temple. I loved going to temple as a girl; it was such a grand and beautiful place. I felt then as though I could take anything that troubled me and leave it there. I would sit for hours and feel myself enveloped in its beauty and holiness. I would dance and feel Adonai relieve me of my fears in the sweet dance offerings of my feet.

As you know, females were not allowed into the inner sanctum, but I loved to sit as close as I could to hear whatever I might, though I was often shooed away by indignant priests and Pharisees. At home, I admit I continued this dangerous habit whenever the holy men came to visit my father. Particularly the day they came to discuss my nuptial agreement. I know my father did not believe I was cleaning the door—

the way I landed on my ear when he opened it unexpectedly. I will never forget the way the rabbi looked at me—his eyes held such burning contempt for a simple, curious little girl.

But then my mother glided into the room with a platter of her famous raisin cakes. Her eyes dutifully downcast, she asked permission to speak. With mouths full of placating cakes, the men grumbled their consent. As I scrambled out of the way, my mother explained that while she was pregnant with me, in a dream an angel had come to her saying that my name was to be Shimoni, "she who hears." My father, looking as though he was hearing this revelation for the first time, was quickly engaged with a piece of tenderly placed raisin cake. She went on to tell them what a good girl I was and of the hours I spent each week taking care of our family friend, the widow Mordecai. "You remember the widow Mordecai?" she said. "She never got over the loss of her two sons in the massacre of the children at Bethlehem at the hands of Herod the so-called Great." What a wise woman she was, my mother. That was all it took to deftly lead the old rabbi into a discourse on how he had inherited Mordecai's cloak. He rambled on until the platter produced no more raisin cakes, my eavesdropping had been forgotten, and my fate had been sealed when I was thirteen with a betrothal contract to Jedediah the cloth merchant.

It seemed so unfair to me that the temple had received all the proceeds from the sale of Widow Mordecai's house and how the scribes and their minions acted so magnanimously each time they delivered the widow's meager pension. Father said it was all done according to the letter of the Law, and the widow felt they favored her by delivering it; at least she did not have to beg. Such a kind soul, she would tell me with those deep-seeing eyes that her lot in life was exactly what she deserved; with no sons and no husband, she was at the mercy of her distant relatives and the generosity of the temple. I had a few conversations with Adonai about that, I'll tell you. . . .

I think the last time I saw her anywhere near happy was at my wedding seven years ago. She had given me a lepton, the smallest of coins in size and worth. As she pressed it into my hand, she said, "Little Shimoni, this is all that is left of my bridal dowry. In this world it means very little, but it has symbolized for my heart the greatest years of my happiness. May it bring you great happiness too, my dear, many sons, and a good husband in this merchant Jedediah."

Oh, my wedding day. I was in such fear, but my parents were convinced that it was a good match and concerned that I was almost two years past the marriageable age. They spared no expense in celebrating, and what a banquet it was; all my favorites. I will never forget the first time I met my betrothed. He seemed so old. But in truth he was such a good man. He was a cloth merchant who loved his work, and after a time I think he loved me. You know, I think he would not have minded if we had been given female children along with some handsome sons . . . but it was not to be. Six years of marriage, and I could produce no children for him. He never shamed me for it, though, and how I loved him for that. The widow's lepton had indeed brought me a good man.

After my parents died, he would hold me for hours. And then one night when I was inconsolable over their absence and the absence of children from my womb, he did the most striking thing. He went to the sacred place in our home and brought out the tasseled holy scroll, and he began to read to me. My beloved husband, in the fullness of the evening, in the privacy of our chambers, brought out the Scriptures and began reading the Angel Wing Psalm to me: "You who dwell in the shelter of Adonai, who abide in the shadow of God, say to Adonai my refuge, my God in whom I trust. . . . And God will rescue you and give you angels to lift you up and guard you wherever you go" (Psalm 91:1-2, 11). And then, though forbidden, Jedediah handed me the holy Writ. "Suffer not a woman to touch the holy Writ," I had said. "Bah!" said he.

I felt as though my fingertips had turned to gold. I was in the inner sanctum of the temple holding the Holy of Holies, and I heard in my heart all the things I had longed to hear as a girl. Something happened to both of us that night. We had broken the letter of the Law, but it was as if the Law was transformed by love that night. I did feel that night that there were angels sent to care for me; that they had inspired my husband into finding me worthy to hear and touch the holy Word of God. It was a rule broken to heal a broken heart, and it worked. And then I danced for him.

Not long after, about a week before Passover, Jedediah went to the temple to pay his tax. When he came home, he said he had caught a chill and was frustrated because he hadn't been able to get through to the moneychanger in order to pay his tax. Those were the last words I ever heard him speak. Some said it was one of the foreigners in the city who brought the disease that took my husband's life. Others whispered that like my barrenness, it was just another sign of God's disfavor upon me.

All I know is that after I tried to rouse him that afternoon and could not, and all the healers' herbs worked to no avail, I knew that my life would end with his. As I went to hold his anguished and clenched hands one last time, I found two one-half shekels and one bronze lepton. He would have used the lepton to pay the moneychangers for the conversion tax. As I held the lepton, I remembered the night he had read to me from the Psalms and we both had been changed by his compassion. After we put the scroll away and lay there quietly, he had asked me, "A lepton for your thoughts?"

I told him then I was wondering about the Messiah. It seemed like now would be a good time for him to come, what with the world in such political turmoil and so many warmongers in power. I told him it felt as though men in power knew how to do nothing but go to war, and we could do with a good chariot of fire to help the Messiah burn away some of the foolishness in our leaders. Jedediah had chuckled and told me of the man he had heard speaking down at the temple, an itinerate rabbi who had been roaming the countryside. He said though the man smelled of fish, he taught Torah as Jedediah had never heard it taught before. His name was Jesu or something, and Jed had thought he was remarkable. But this Jesu had no army, just a ragtag bunch of homeless people, it would seem, who had no weapons and no way to secure the city, let alone change the world. He'd already angered the scribes, who were busy spreading rumors that he was a crazy magician, not to be trusted. But Jedediah was intrigued, I could tell. Oh, how I long for my thoughtful husband now.

After my year of mourning was complete and Jedediah's brother could no longer care for another mouth in his house, I had no options. I had a distant cousin, my only relative living in Bethany, and I decided to walk there to see if they would take me. So I set off with all of my worldly possessions, consisting primarily of the clothes on my back. It was the time when the city of my birth was full of Passover pilgrims. There had been a strange procession the week before, and as I walked by the temple for one last look, dried-up palm branches crackled under my feet. Something was afoot; I could feel it in the air.

How I had loved to go to the temple when I was a girl. No binding veils to trip me up as I danced on those holy stones. God was strong and powerful for me then and knew my innermost thoughts. *Where are you now, Adonai?* As I approached the temple, I could see clusters of scribes and Pharisees standing about, all quite agitated. Instinctively I went to make sure I was fully covered, and as my hand went into my pocket, I felt them: the widow Mordecai's wedding gift and Jedediah's temple tax, the two leptons; beside my memories and the clothes on my back, they were all that was left of my life. I could see lines of people in front of the temple treasury chattering excitedly. What wealth and treasures they offered. I had nothing to give save the two leptons, hardly enough to buy a piece of day-old bread, perhaps my last piece of bread.

I dropped the two coins amid the richer gold and silver—for a moment I felt as if my whole life was drawing out of me—an unseen offering to an unseen and long unfelt God; the tax of a barren and useless widow's life, dull bronze against the gold and silver of the world's rich offerings. Feeling as fragile as an unbaked pot, I made my way to the end of the courtyard, passing by a ragtag bunch of people smelling of fish. Pulling my shawl about me, I saw that they were looking at me, which scared me. I turned to flee, but as I passed by them, I heard the man in the middle say, "This poor widow has put in more than all who have contributed to the treasury." My steps hesitated. "For they have all put in money they could spare, but she in her poverty has put in everything she possessed." I stopped and looked at him, and his eyes were filled with such compassion as I had not seen since Jedediah was alive. But there was more; I had never seen him before in my life, yet his face was so familiar. How could he have known of my last two leptons? And to have honored my emptiness, it was as if he saw inside me. And then, I tell you he recited the very verse that Jedediah had read to me on that distant, loving night: "You who dwell in the shelter of Adonai, who abide in the shadow of God, say to Adonai my refuge, my God in whom I trust. . . . And God will rescue you and give you angels to lift you up and guard you wherever you go."

Obviously I survived and lived to tell this tale. My name is Shimoni, and I did hear him that day in the temple courtyard, and I was changed forever. Shalom and amen.

A version of this sermon was preached on April 6, 2003, at Washington Park United Church of Christ, Denver, Colorado. This sermon is an imagined-story sermon told in first person. It is based on the account of the widow in the Gospel of Mark, whom Jesus witnessed contributing to the temple treasury more that anyone else, as she put in all that she had.

16

Overshadowed by the Power of God

Portia Wills Lee

LUKE 1:24-56

Mary said to the angel, "How can this be, since I am a virgin?" The angel said to her, "The Holy Spirit will come upon you, and the power of the Most High will overshadow you; therefore the child to be born will be holy; he will be called Son of God." (Luke 1:34-35, NRSV)

My paternal grandmother, Portia Wills, was a phenomenal, multi-talented, and multitasking career woman. If she were living today, she would be very close to one hundred years old. During the late 1960s and early 1970s, she owned and operated several businesses in the segregated South, including a women's health spa, where she was a licensed masseuse. She taught women exercise, health, nutrition, and beauty classes. I was always intrigued by this African American woman who was able to defy the climate of her day—the segregated South, Jim Crow laws, and undereducation—to become successful in all her entrepreneurial endeavors.

I have always pondered over the courage, strength, and tenacity that so many women possess to beat the probabilities and to become everything God has called them to be. Key examples include women of the Scriptures and those recorded in the history/herstory books: Miriam, Zipporah, Hannah, Esther, Ruth, the woman with an issue of blood, the Samaritan woman, Lydia, to name a few. Furthermore, there were Sojourner Truth, Harriett Tubman, Jarena Lee, Zora Neale Hurston, Rosa Parks, and Wilma Rudolph.

Likewise, the call narrative of Jesus' mother, Mary, fascinates me. In Mary's story, we are given principles of what it takes to be a powerful woman used by God. Mary was a young, poor female. God chose Mary for an important act of obedience. The angel Gabriel gave Mary the message that God had a divine purpose for her life: to give birth to the Messiah. Mary did not understand, and she immediately prayed by asking, "How can this be, since I do not know a man?"

We may feel that our ability, place of nativity, experience, or education makes us an unlikely candidate for God's service. However, we should not limit God's choices. God can use us if we trust God. God uses women in spite of the conditions of the day to make a difference in our communities, nation, and the world. Scriptures give witness to God using Mary and countless other women. The records of herstory may not give written testimony of the unsung stories of women like my grandmother, but their legacies of how God overshadowed them will be passed on for countless generations.

God's favor does not always bring automatic success, wealth, or fame. God's blessing on Mary led to much pain: her peers perhaps ridiculed her, her fiancé came close to leaving her, she conceivably brought shame upon her family, she was forced to move to another nation, and her son was rejected and murdered. Still, the world's only hope would come through her son, which is why Mary has been called "the favored one" by countless generations! Her submission led to our salvation and taught us God's love. If sorrow weighs us down and dims our hope, we should think of Mary and wait patiently for God to finish enacting God's plan for our lives.

Mary found strength and courage to be used by God because she prayed, because she was overshadowed by God's power, and because she developed a relationship with a partner who knew God. Like God used Mary, God can use us when we pray if we allow ourselves to become overshadowed by the power of God and if we partner with people God places in our lives.

Prayer is our avenue for communicating with God, to tell God those matters in our hearts and to listen as God speaks to us. God wants us to have an intentional prayer life in which we communicate to God how much we **A**dore God, **C**onfess our sins, **T**hank God for our many blessings, and Supplicate for others and self; ACTS is the key to an effective prayer life. When we ACT by seeking God, God then acts on our behalf by answering our prayers.

There are times when our prayers may be one thought or a mere sentence. In Mary's one-sentence prayer ("How can this be, since I do not know a man?"), she confessed her ignorance of how God could use her. The most trusting believers have questioned God at some point in their lives. We could also ask if Mary's seemingly disbelief reflected a sinful disposition on her part. Our answer: no! The text seems to suggest that Mary's disbelief was rooted in her inability to fully understand the capability of what had been proposed. She did not say that it was impossible.

It is through prayer that we come to know the power of God that creates, sustains, forgives, blesses, and empowers us! It is in Mary's prayer, as she confesses her ignorance, that she shows how she came to know that all things are possible with God. Mary realized that it was not her relations with a man that would make the impossible possible, but her relationship with God. God always has the final word in every episode of human drama.

It is not when we have been with a man or a woman that brings the miracle of God to pass, but it is when we have been with God that we are blessed with God's power. That power overshadows us and helps us do what is impossible without God. We come to understand that it is God who uses humanity to be a blessing to us. It was God's power that Jesus felt leaving him when the woman with the issue of blood touched him! It was God's power that called Jairus's daughter back to life! It was God's power that forgave the Samaritan woman! It was God's power that gave Jesus strength to endure the excruciating pain on the cross! It was God's power that raised Jesus from the grave! It is through the power of God that we are able to say, "I can do all things through [Christ] who strengthens me" (Philippians 4:13 NRSV)! It is the same power that gave my grandmother the strength and courage to strive for success in spite of the obstacles she faced in the South.

God's power overshadowed Mary. It was at this point that the angel Gabriel reminded Mary that her cousin, Elizabeth, was with child in her old age. Mary went to Cousin Elizabeth's house, for she understood she needed the wisdom of someone who knew what the power of God can do. God assigned Elizabeth to be Mary's partner for the mission. The common interests that Mary and Cousin Elizabeth share is that they both were in a season of their lives when conception should have been impossible. They both were overshadowed by God, who enabled them to bear children with a divine mission from God for the world. The sons these two women birthed became partners in God's divine plan for the world. Cousin Elizabeth's son, John the Baptist, was the forerunner for Mary's son, Jesus the Messiah.

The Scriptures give witness that God never gives us a mission without giving us a partner to assist in carrying out the divine plan. In the Christian writings, we discover that Jesus had John the Baptist and the disciples, Paul had Silas and Timothy, Lydia had her prayer partners, and Aquila had Priscilla. My grandmother had her church, family, and friends who encouraged her. Partners generally offer each other prayer, support, encouragement, enlightenment, and empowerment for the mission. Usually, when one partner becomes weakened or discouraged, the other can remind him or her of God's power and words that will inspire them to keep going—words such as "God didn't bring you this far to leave you," "God will never leave nor forsake you," "God is our very present help in time of trouble," and so on.

My grandmother Portia partnered with women to teach them health care. She partnered with women to complete wardrobe outfits because she was also a hat designer and hat maker. Mother Portia would design hats to fit a woman's style and personality. At times, women would bring their hats back to their creative partner because a hat was damaged. She offered them support and encouraged them. As a child, I loved watching her take damaged hats and put them back together. While a pot of water was boiling, she would take the covering off the hat. She would then take the straw or binding and place it over the water to carefully work with it, reshaping it into its original design or to a new design. When women picked up their hats, they expressed such joy over how my grandmother made the seemingly impossible possible. My grandmother's ability came because her life had been overshadowed by the power of God. She knew that all things are possible with God.

When we are in relationship with God and allow God to overshadow our lives, we can see that the impossible is possible. I am so glad that Mary allowed God's power to overshadow her so we could have a partner named Jesus who is our friend, a friend who loves, protects, provides, forgives, heals, sustains, and blesses. Jesus, who gives light in darkness, who gives us hope, is the Bread of Life, is the Truth, the Way, and the Life. Jesus, who gives us life and life more abundantly! Amen.

A longer version of this sermon was preached on August 21, 2005, at Trinity Tabernacle Baptist Church, Mableton, Georgia.

17

Mary's Song[1]

Gayll Phifer-Houseman

LUKE 1:26-56

"I am the Lord's servant," Mary answered. "May it be to me as you have said."
Then the angel left her. (Luke 1:38, NIV)

How long? It's a good question for the Advent season. "How long
until school's out?" my daughter demands. "How many shopping
days left?" "When will we leave for our trip?" "How long until the
visiting relatives go home?"

How long? is a question of longing, even need. It's a question of
impatience and eagerness for something good to begin or of desperation and desire for something difficult to end.

Our culture puts most of its focus on the shopping and wrapping
and decorating and baking before Christmas arrives. But Advent
shouldn't be a time when we rush around amassing piles of presents
or arranging faux reindeer on the lawn. Instead, Advent is supposed
to be a time to slow down and reconnect with, rather than run from,
the world's deep longing for restoration and justice, healing, forgiveness, peace on earth, goodwill toward all humanity.

Obviously, waiting for God and God's redemption isn't as festive as
decking the halls or toasting the season. And yet God promises us that
as we reconnect with a longing for God and the Good, we will celebrate more profoundly God's salvation that comes on Christmas Day.

How long? It was the big question in first-century Palestine too.
The world's groan for justice, for help from on high has been going on
for centuries. The Jewish people bitterly resented Roman occupation.

Like sharecroppers on their own land, they paid heavy taxes to Rome and were governed by puppet dictators who actively collaborated with the Romans. To the Jewish people, God seemed to have lapsed into 450 years of silence. "How long, O Lord?" was a question on everyone's mind.

And then, *bang!* God breaks through and sends a messenger to a teenage girl in a tiny hick town on the edge of nowhere:

"Con-gra-tu-la-tions, Mary! It's your *lucky* day! God's on your side!"

"Uh, he is?"

"Yes! And now for a limited time only, the God of the universe is answering the cry of your people and you—yes, you, Mary—you are the lucky recipient of the Mother-of-God Sweepstakes!"

"Me? But I never even filled out an entry form."

"*Not* a problem! We've got that covered. Your mission (should you choose to accept it) is to allow yourself to become pregnant with God and give birth to the Savior of the world! (Dealer fees, tax, and license not included, offer not available in all areas, no room at the inn, death threats and refugee status may apply)."

Bewildering, isn't it? We wait, we long, we groan for change, help, answers, a shot at redemption, and then when we least expect it, where we least expect it, to whom one would least expect it, God breaks in with a personal invitation to participate in the reclamation of the universe—God's ultimate answer to our cry of "How long?"

It's always like that. God's answers to the world's problems often come as unexpected interruptions in the lives of normal people who are just minding their own business. All Mary needs here is the ability to completely suspend disbelief and the courage to risk everything (her future, her reputation, her physical safety, her whole life) on the offer.

We need to reframe our picture of Mary from some starry-eyed, blissed-out beauty to a startled but spunky young woman of revolutionary courage and ferocious faith. To be unwed and pregnant in her culture was not the common, ho-hum slip-up that it is in our day—God is literally proposing to get Mary into trouble. In order to give birth to Jesus, Mary had to risk not only being misunderstood and ridiculed but also rejected, abandoned, exiled, or stoned to death by her family, her fiancé, and her community. She had to be willing to put everything on the line in order to participate in God's work in the world. Accepting the mission to bear the Messiah meant Mary's entire life was set on a collision course with sadistic despots like Herod the Great and Caesar Augustus. Within months, she and Joseph and their newborn son were on Herod's most-wanted list. (No baby shower for this kid.) Saying yes to Gabriel set in motion a life-threatening chain of events in Mary's life and in the world from which there was no going back—an action adventure worthy of *Mission Impossible III*.

And yet, in spite of the risks, after her initial confusion at how all this would work, Mary responds with openness ("I am the Lord's servant"), excitement, and probably some fear (she hurried to Elizabeth's), and even exuberance and exhilaration. She sings, "My soul glorifies the Lord and my spirit rejoices in God my Savior, for he has been mindful of the humble state of his servant. From now on all generations will call me blessed, for the Mighty One has done great things for me—holy is his name. His mercy extends to those who fear him, from generation to generation" (Luke 1:46-50, NIV).

Why? What has God done that's so great? What does this mercy look like? Just this: that God has invited us—allowed you and me—messed up, broken, frail, and clueless as we are, to participate (like Mary) in the world's redemption. And it just doesn't get any better than that—this is a Christmas present worth having. We all are invited to participate in God's work in the world. The angel comes to us all.

How? The cover of a news magazine calls out to us; something we see on TV troubles our sleep. We bump into an old friend who reminds us of an old commitment. We hear a sermon, read a book, hear a statistic, or engage in a conversation that we can't get out of our head. These are not random encounters. God speaks to us through the world's cries. Anything that troubles us has the seed of a calling in it. And that calling crystallizes as we make room for that unlikely angel's message during a season like Advent.

How are we responding to God's current invitation in our lives? Could an angel get a word in edgewise in our lives? We can be so busy, distracted, previously committed or padded with comfort that a whole heavenly host couldn't get our attention if they tried. Does Gabriel's message seem like good news, or have we put limits on the parts of our life that God is allowed to interrupt? The truth is, too often we put God in the God-box and expect that God will not mess with our boyfriend or girlfriend, our career or college major, our retirement income, our family planning, our health, or our relationships with parents, kids, or spouse. We hesitate to answer God's call until all the little ducks line up neatly so that we know the next step is safe.

Here's God's word for us today: Don't get hung up on these things! Advent is short, and Emmanuel will be here soon! There are only a few days left to prepare! Every attempt to manage God's work in your life or to write your own life's story is a failed project. It has been said that a birth isn't something you do, as much as something you submit to. And it is only as we echo Mary's words of surrender that we find our true story in God's story.

Mark and I experienced an unmistakable call from God to adopt our four children—in spite of our manifold limitations, across a world-sized divide. And they, in turn, accepted an invitation from God to take the huge risk to embrace us as parents, in spite of the fact we were completely unknown to them and absolutely underqualified to raise Ethiopian children. Even after five years, we don't know what we're doing! I wanted my ducks all in a row, but my ducks are running around all over the place, and I've been asked to do things I'm so bad at that I can't even remember what a comfort zone is! In fact, I've come to believe that if it doesn't have "crisis" in front of it, it's not really "management."

But what does that matter? *God* is in our midst, and we know we have all been invited to take part in a small piece of his extraordinary purposes in the world. We know as a family, as a church, that we are highly favored. "For the mighty God has done great things for me, and holy is his name."

I wouldn't want anyone to miss out on God's presence, power, and calling in life during this Advent season. I wouldn't want us to gain all the gifts in the mall and miss out on the adventure of a lifetime. So, let's leave the fruitcake and faux deer behind and use these weeks as a time of quieting our spirits in preparation for his coming so that we do not miss the angel's visit, the surprising call. So we can indeed say with Mary, "I am the Lord's servant. Let it be to me as you have said."

A longer version of this sermon was preached at The River Church Community, San Jose, California, December 10, 2006.

1. Portions of this sermon were inspired and informed by another woman preacher, Loretta Ross, *Letters from the Holy Ground: Seeing God Where You Are* (Franklin, WI: Sheed and Ward, 2000), 180–81.

18

Blessed Are the Breasts

Zaida Maldonado Pérez

LUKE 11:27-28

"Blessed is the womb that bore you and the breasts that nursed you!" But he said, "Blessed rather are those who hear the word of God and obey it!" (Luke 11:27-28, NRSV)

These verses, found exclusively in the Gospel of Luke, are the only ones where a woman is said to have stood up boldly in the midst of a crowd and, with the might of her lungs, stated what was on her mind, or, in this case, in her heart. This is also one of those passages where God's intention for women *and* men is clearly and eloquently spelled out: urgent words, words full of promise, immensely profound.

Now, if you followed the text closely, you're probably asking yourself, "Why?" Why choose such a text to talk about the role and importance of women in God's reign? Let's face it; the woman in this text doesn't appear to be very bright! I mean, here we have Jesus; he's just made a mute man speak, and a big crowd has gathered around him now, and he's expounding, discoursing on the great truths of God's kingdom, power, and authority. All is quiet, and all eyes are on Jesus. And then, all of a sudden, this woman comes out of nowhere and starts yelling something about body parts—bearing wombs and nursing breasts! "Blessed is the womb that bore you and the breasts that nursed you," she yells. And, well, I can just hear the men in the crowd right now. I can hear her husband, if she had one: "Hm, hm, hm! Juuust like a woman!"

If you were a woman, back in the first century, and even before then, whether you were Greek, Roman, or Jewish, your personhood or worth was intricately tied to your physical body (they were big on biology back then). Greek physicians and many a philosopher taught that women were created imperfectly, that they were imperfect males. For Greco-Romans it was the male, the uncircumcised male, who was held up as the perfect image of the gods both in body and in intellect. The woman, however, was generally considered weak, unpredictable, and given to emotions. And so males were thought to be naturally superior to females. And, because she was inferior, the man was to rule over her.[1] That's just how things were. Now, though Jews thought of, and treated, their women in a better light, they were prone to thinking of them as temptresses. Men, especially young boys, were told to be on their guard, because evil, conniving women could drag them to the pit of hell.[2]

Women's purpose in life was also tied to their body. Jewish, Greek, or Roman women were expected to get married, tend the home, and bear their husband some children, especially boys. This was their vocation, their calling. This unknown woman was only expressing the prevalent idea that a woman's total worth was attached to how many children she was able to bear and how productive her children turned out to be. "Blessed is the womb that bore you and the breasts that nursed you!"

Ah, but listen to Jesus' response: "Blessed are they who hear the word of God and keep it." Jesus is acknowledging this woman, and through her, all women for who they are as persons and children of God. Jesus is telling her that the nonperson image she has been taught to believe about herself is no longer valid. "Rather," he says, "blessed is the one who will hear and follow God's word"—that's the honored one, the blessed one in God's reign! Neither role, nor gender, nor status has anything to do with whom God loves and whom God chooses to call and nothing to do with the type of ministry God chooses for any one of us. God loves us because God wills, and calls whom God wills, for whatever God wills! We don't determine that—God does! And God is God!

You know, I'd like to think that woman thought deeply about what Jesus said. I'd like to think that instead of going home feeling embarrassed, stupid, or ashamed, she went home a new woman—a liberated woman, a woman whose identity is not tied to what her body can or cannot do but to what God in Christ has already done for her.

I have to say that as a woman, and *puertorriqueña,* I love God's reign; by that, I mean the ongoing glimpses of God's grace even, and most especially, amid all the struggles to overcome cultural, linguistic, racial, and economic barriers. It's so beautiful and wonderfully *loco* at the same time!

> Only in God's reign does Christ die a criminal's death on a cross instead of easily donning a crown and proclaiming himself King.
> In God's reign, Christ sits and eats with sinners, forgives the outcast, and offends conservatives by healing on the Sabbath.
> In God's reign, the first is last and the last is first.
> Only in God's reign are women and men equally loved and equally called to serve in whatever capacity God chooses for them. They may not always be allowed to exercise that calling, but it does not mean that God did not call them!
> In God's reign, *mujeres y hombres* are called to pool their talents and resources to develop their God-given potentials and be examples and instruments of that "new thing" God is always doing in our midst.
> In God's reign, things are as they should be—topsy-turvy, upside down, inside out—and this is good and right!

Today God continues to call women of all races and places—not because there are no men to do God's work. Thank God there are, and in fact, we need more! God calls us because, when it comes to God's children, God has no gender preference—we all fall short of the glory of God!

The better equipped women are, the better we can deal with the tough questions and issues in the home, church, and our communities. And, given the complexity of the problems we're dealing with today— we need all the help we can get!

Because I know that women are pretty much built of enduring God-given stuff that makes us who we are, I think it is pretty safe to venture that there are some wonderful, powerful, strong, energetic, loving, caring, intelligent, go-get-'em kinds of women in this place! Can you imagine Asbury without them? We are blessed by their presence and example. Ask any one of them about the incredible things they have had to endure, the struggles, abuse, and pain they've encountered and overcome, the obstacles they have crossed to get to where they are and where they want to be, and what you'll find there are some courageous, incredibly intelligent women. Nursing warriors, I like to call them—women capable of being sensitive yet strong—G.I. moms, grandmas, aunts, and daughters.

Paul reminds us in Ephesians that, as church, we aren't complete without each other and without each other's gifts and needs. Perhaps our presence or work goes unnoticed every once in a while. And, maybe we'll continue to be seen just a little below the standard for some outside our church community. But, I like to dream, and I am positive there is an angel in heaven recording everything that has been and will be left out of history's annals about women's contributions to, with, and for God's reign. See it with me! There's a "who honored God" book in heaven, and many names are in it! And there's a "who stood up for your sister and acknowledged her gifts and aided her, somehow, to be a greater blessing in God's reign" book; and men of Asbury Theological Seminary, your names are in it!

Church, we need each other. No gift can be wasted. No talent undeveloped. A mind is a terrible thing to waste. "Blessed is the womb that bore you and the breasts that nursed you," she yelled. And Jesus replied, "Blessed rather is the woman and man who will hear God's Word and keep it!"

A version of this sermon was first preached at Christ the King Congregational Church (UCC), St. Louis, Missouri, on September 21, 1997 (Pastor Tony Smith). It was preached again at a women's event called "Amazed by Grace," Fifth Annual Women of Color Conference by the Center for Emerging Female Leadership, Bronx, New York, in 1999. It was also preached in Orlando at a local congregation (Rev. Charles Baxter, 2003) and at the Orlando campus of Asbury Theological Seminary, on October 12, 2004.

1. See *Women's Life in Greece and Rome: A Source Book in Translation,* comp. Mary R. Lefkowitz and Maureen B. Fant (Baltimore: John Hopkins University Press, 1992), 38.

2. See, e.g., Proverbs 7 and 9.

19

Spiritual Alchemy

Sakena D. Young-Scaggs

LUKE 12:49-56

"You hypocrites! You know how to interpret the appearance of earth and sky, but why do you not know how to interpret the present time?" (Luke 12:56, NRSV)

The message today takes its cue from the environmental shifts happening all over the world, climate change. The texts read in your hearing today are not so soft on the ears: the prophetic voice of Isaiah 5:1-7; Psalm 82; and Luke 12:49-56. Throughout Marsh Chapel's National Summer Preaching Series, the preachers, teachers, and prophets who have stood in this pulpit called for a climate change.[1] Today we end one season and begin another. Scholars, students, and parents are scrambling to prepare to reenter schools and institutions of higher learning. A climate change: change of space, place, and routines.

Our text echoes our condition in Christ's teaching for us today, asking us whether we are ready for a climate change. In our Gospel text, the good doctor Luke provides us with a clear picture of the Messiah's teachings, parables, and acts. In our particular text, we find "JC"[2] teaching on the way to Jerusalem. He tells them, "Something is coming," and after it arrives nothing will be the same. This Jesus is not gentle Jesus, Lamb of God, or Baby Jesus who wouldn't harm a fly. This Jesus tells his disciples not to be afraid and then gives them every reason to be terrified. "Be not afraid" does not mean "sit back and relax as God gives you the kingdom." Rather, it is more like a commander telling soldiers, "Take courage, the battle is ours," before they engage in fierce combat.[3]

Christ paints a picture of discord and ensuing conflict as he journeys toward the cross. He expresses his inner challenge, the coming changes, the painstaking event he knows lies before him that he wishes were already over.

Despite looming certainty of undesirable events, Christ teaches and preaches preparation and consciousness—radical! Christ's voice in Luke 12 says, "Brace yourself! You're about to go through something that hurts. But brace yourself! A storm is coming, and you're not gonna like it!" If we need a reference point, just think about those annual physical exams. We say to ourselves: brace yourself! Christ interrogates our human ability to discern and interpret the times, present and those coming. Are we able to see what's before us? Can we see it coming?

Have we braced ourselves for supernatural encounters and foreboding events to come? Certainly we, humanity, are brilliant and knowledgeable and possess technology that soars across the information highway. But can we tune out the natural and tune in spiritually? When all the books are closed; CNN, Headline News, and Sports Center have signed off; Wall Street is still; all the power strips are flipped; the servers are all down; every cell phone bar is on low; every wireless has lost connectivity; and the superhighway of life is still for just a millisecond, are we able to draw on supernatural power, on our spiritual connection to God Almighty?

Today, this question is as critical and scathing as the ones Christ uttered in Luke 12:56. It has such an ominous, prophetic, and mysterious heaviness. Perhaps we want to dismiss the prophetic voice as invalid, as supernatural mumbo jumbo, another conspiracy theorist or perhaps mad scientist, we are so reasonable and rational. We want to dismiss prophetic voices as on-the-edge activists, as another one of those religious zealots or even tree-hugging, political attention seekers tired of running for office. We dismiss many who proposed climate change by putting them in any one of these categories. Beloved, I'm here today to declare there is a storm coming, and we cannot ignore it. There are changes taking place in the physical and in the spiritual realms, around the globe, around our homes, and I pray today, also within our hearts and souls.

With a fervent voice Christ demands an answer! Are we ready to step back from our human reason and rationalism and open our eyes to see with the vision of the Spirit? The actual weather will change. Floods, storms, earthquakes, and global hothouse effect—those are plainly before our very eyes. But Christ requires us to move beyond the physical, beyond the natural into the supernatural, to seek spiritual readiness for things to come. As people of faith, our very belief is based on elements outside the natural realm, outside the realm of rationality. Think about it. We believe in unprecedented events over two thousand years ago that scientists still are trying to explain. We believe in a boy, born of a virgin, who grew up incognito as a migrant woodworker in Egypt. We believe that in his thirties he embraced his second career as Messiah, walked on water, healed the sick, gave blind people sight, brought forth a religious revolution, was crucified, died, and was buried, then rose again from the dead. We believe he ascended into heaven, but not before leaving a mandate that humanity must be ready for him to come again. Yes, our faith, our belief itself, is outside the realm of the ordinary. If we believe in these things we must also believe in the impact this same belief can have on one's personal life and the power it wields to exact blessings on the lives of others. Believers have the ability to bring forth something new; to transform the old, the mundane, and the common into something innovative and extraordinary.

I want to tell you about a very natural act that has helped me connect with my supernatural faith. It's the ministry of hospitality. One component of it is food. I have become queen of quick, quality, healthy food. Yet, in contrast, for hours in my spare time, I study recipes and spend days putting together menus for special events and to survive. I love to create something new out of what appears to be nothing. In college, I would have ramen and mac-and-cheese cook-offs in dorm kitchens, just to see who could make the best creation and stretch something out of what appeared to be nothing.

Cooking is like that: you start with a few ingredients and you lay them out—the dry with the dry, the wet with the wet, the solids and the diced. As each ingredient interacts with another, something almost miraculous happens—it comes together to create something new. My daughters and I call it "kitchen alchemy."

There is a similar kind of alchemy in the Spirit. Ingredients for personal spiritual alchemy are stirred up in the Spirit and shaped by the hand of God. They are forged in the flames of a very real life in our global society, a very real life in local communities and intimately real in our own homes and hearts.

Some of us stay in our safe Sims world:[4] simulated worlds, simulated relationships, and simulated passions. The truth is that there are real changes to face every day. When one rises at the cost of another, we need a climate change. When homes are swept away physically by war, fire, and famine as a result of societal selfishness, we need a climate change. When freedom of thought and personhood are bound up by class and social caste; when American slavery oozes back into society through the penal system;[5] when relationships are bound by sensuality, utilitarian networking, and monetary materialism, we need a climate change.

The social gospel of Jesus Christ demands a climate change! So brace yourself! Get ready in the Spirit! You may have already experienced a personal encounter with God, with Jesus, and the Holy Spirit. You may have stopped your rat-race life already to say, "Here I am, Lord—I commit my soul, my heart, and my gifts to thee." You may have prepared in the Spirit for the social, adversarial, and opportunistic discord and disapproval that will surely come. You may have taken time out and entered into heavenly cyberspace, laying out all the alchemic elements: through prayer, the Internet; through praise, the fiber optics; through communal hospitality and regular worship—the hardware. Do you have good virus protection? Now that's the Word of God! It will protect you from any infiltration by demonic enemies. Oh, have you stored up your heavenly treasures? That would be your flash drives and back-up disks. Then you might just be ready for a bit of supernatural cyberspace, spiritual alchemy, prepared and conscious to connect with the promise of salvation.

Bishop John R. Bryant calls it a "Jesus Connection,"[6] a connection that heals, teaches, provides, cares, restores, befriends, liberates, empowers, and, yes, saves! It saves us from sin and sometimes saves us from our very selves. Open your hearts. Get ready to experience a new climate of love unbound! Get ready for hope without end. Get ready for a relationship with God on whom you know you can depend. Are you ready for a climate change? Good. I can see it coming, and I'm ready too. Amen.

A longer version of this sermon was first preached at Marsh Chapel on August 19, 2007, at the close of the Marsh Chapel National Summer Preaching Series and as a departing sermon to Young-Scaggs's post as associate dean of Marsh Chapel; the original version can be found at www.bu.edu/chapel in the sermon archive.

1. The Marsh Chapel National Summer Preaching Series, inaugural year 2007, is an eight-part series of preachers from around the globe held annually at Boston University. See also www.bu.ed.chapel.

2. "JC" means Jesus Christ; I call him "JC;" we're personal and intimate like that.

3. Worship Planning Helps, 2007 (Nashville: General Board of Discipleship of the United Methodist Church, www.umcworship.org).

4. In 2000, a computer game titled "Sims" was released. In the game, players escape into a simulated electronic world. See http://thesims.ea.com.

5. In the Constitution of the United States of America, Article XIII, slavery and involuntary servitude were banished "except as a punishment for crime whereof the party shall have been duly convicted." In a nation where the "duly convictions" are often suspect, the implications are socially oppressive at best and a return to the draconian practice of slavery under the guise of the prison industrial complex.

6. John R. Bryant, "Living a Connected Life," in *The Anvil: Living Well Every Day,* Annual Resources Guide, Quadrennial (Nashville: Council of Bishops of the African Episcopal Church, 2005).

20

At the Table

Liala Ritsema Beukema

LUKE 14:1, 7-14

"But when you give a banquet, invite the poor, the crippled, the lame, and the blind. And you will be blessed, because they cannot repay you, for you will be repaid at the resurrection of the righteous." (Luke 14:13-14, NRSV)

Some of my best times growing up were those occasions when the whole clan gathered for a family dinner. Aunts and uncles, cousins and friends, and oftentimes the unexpected new acquaintance all gathered around the table. With all those people collected, it was impossible for everyone to have a place at the big table. The "big table," as we called it, was reserved for the adults. The rest of us were relegated to the "kids' table," often times a rickety old card table or two, barely disguised by stained linens and mismatched silverware. Both sides of my family had "big tables," but I liked the one on my father's side best, because in that circle I was the second oldest grandchild, so I got to sit with the adults more often than at my mother's family gatherings, where I was third from the bottom.

Jesus was invited to a dinner. And when he arrived, it became clear that he had been invited to sit in the designated hot seat at this banquet at the "big table." The very fact that he had been invited to the home of a Pharisee was enough to pique curiosity. It had become obvious that the relationship between Jesus and the Pharisees was politely strained. Jesus, on several occasions, exposed their legalistic and elitist practices and generally irritated these religious leaders. So why would he now be invited to dinner?

Perhaps he was invited so his hosts could make a point, or even discredit him—embarrass him in front of supposedly the most influential people of the community. They did not invite Jesus because they were interested in what he had to say or because they wanted to join with him and follow him. Jesus was aware of the condition of their hearts, and he didn't fall into their trap. Instead, he reversed the embarrassment, not only with his knowledge of the law but also by exposing the unspoken motivations of his hosts and the other guests.

As Jesus was watching people at the feast, he noticed the politicking and scrambling to obtain the best seats at the banquet table—maneuvering to get the best vantage position and working to make sure they had every opportunity to secure their visibility as honored guests. He had been invited to the feast, but there was no room for Jesus at the table.

It's not that different today. There are all kinds of gatherings with tables intended to denote power and prestige. Open the Sunday papers and you will see photos of such occasions on the society pages: smiling faces crowded around some dignitary, politician, or celebrity in hopes of gaining personal attention, or by proximity, validation or value.

We do not always know the motive people have in their desire to befriend us. So Jesus' words to the gathered guests and his words to us are: "Be aware!" Don't take for granted that we know the reasons we have been invited or included. We may believe it is because we have something to contribute or because we have been recognized as a valued or valuable part of the community; we may believe that we are invited to sit at the power table, but we may have fallen into the trap of thinking more of ourselves than we should.

On several occasions, I have received an invitation to participate in special events or gatherings. When I open the envelope and see the beautifully engraved appeal, I get all excited and in the moment think, *Boy, have I really made it! I am going to be hobnobbing with all kinds of important folk. I must really be doing something right.* My friends come by to admire the good fortune I have finally succeeded in making some inroads and receiving the recognition I deserve. When I get to the event, I see that my place card is located on the table closest to the bathroom with all the other folks who represent some quota or represent the minority perspective that, by our presence, enables the hosts and other guests to feel as though they have been inclusive and/or open-minded. I can't tell you how embarrassed I am, how disappointed I am, and then how angry I am—not at those who extend the politically correct invitation, but at myself for my thoughtless participation and perpetuation of a disingenuous and often dehumanizing system.

It may not be as obvious as this. When we identify ourselves as disciples of Jesus, we always are being watched and, like Jesus, being tested. Our friends may call us up and invite us out on the town to see if we have really changed. Others may try to engage us in conversations that are not constructive or loving. We might be offered the deal of a lifetime with conditions and consequences that are great for us, but it conflicts with our sense of what is in the best interest of the whole community. We may not always know the reason people want to include or engage us. So the word of the Lord is that we must know our own hearts and approach each situation with humility and care.

Jesus reminds the guests that if we keep ourselves in perspective, if we remember who we are and whose we are, we will not fall victim to false motives. If we do not feel the need to try and prove ourselves to others or look outside ourselves for a sense of accomplishment or personal worth, we will discover countless opportunities to share ourselves and make a difference in deeply significant and enduring ways.

Jesus also has a word to the hosts of this gathering. We who are guests must be centered and clear about our motivation. So also must we, when opportunities and resources are made available to us, be clear in our motives for distributing and using those gifts. Conventional wisdom encourages us to make good and productive investments. Especially when it seems that we have a limited supply, we want to do whatever it takes to build our personal, political, and social capital.

I can't remember how many times people have suggested it could be in the best financial interest of our community if we had an intentional outreach strategy to our new, wealthier neighbors. Some suggest that we alter our agenda and appearance to become more palatable to those with access to much-needed dollars. In doing so, we are told we would be more financially secure and have resources for our social justice work. What's the harm in so doing if we could accomplish a greater good?

Admittedly, reaching out to wealthy and powerful people has a lot more incentives than the social, political, and economic costs of talking with folks hanging out on street corners on Friday nights. With one we get a lot of affirmation, attention, and money; with the other, we get a lot of flak. But Jesus reminds us of the benefits of reaching out to those who stand outside the banquet hall doors and of the blessings for inviting in those who, for all practical purposes, have nothing to offer us in life.

How do we know that life is the reward? We know because only one feast is pure; only one banquet offers true and sustainable satisfaction. That is the feast of Christ. Jesus speaks the Word, but he is in fact the Word made flesh. By his own life and example, he opened the fellowship hall doors so that all might enter. At Jesus' feast, there is no question about who is the greatest. When we recognize the invitation, we also recognize the admission price Jesus paid so we might enter.

The only way a child could make it to our family's big table was when someone died or left. Spaces were limited. But there always is room at the big table Christ has prepared; his death and resurrection guaranteed space for all. When Jesus calls us to include people who are blind, poor, or lame at his feasts, he does so to remind us that we once were blind, but he opened our eyes; we once were crippled and needed crutches, but he healed our brokenness; we were poor in body and spirit, but he gave us the riches of the kingdom.

If you came here today feeling as if you have been standing on the outside looking in, if you came here today wondering where there is room for you at the big table, if you came here today because you hear the invitation to join in this feast of life, then come. Come to the table of plenty. There is room for you, no strings, no tricks.

A version of this sermon, "Finding Our Place at the Table," was first delivered in 1995 at Church of the Good News, Chicago, and revised/ revisited at Lake View Lutheran Church, Chicago, in September 2007.

21
Stay in the City

EunJoung Joo

LUKE 24:36-49

"I am going to send you what my Father has promised; but stay in the city until you have been clothed with power from on high" (Luke 24:49, NIV)

Sometimes I hear people ask, "Why can't I win my friends to the Lord? Why can't I win my family members to the Lord? Why can't I affect another's life?" To help us answer this question, I'd like to invite us to the day after Jesus Christ was resurrected.

After the crucified Jesus rose from death, people heard that the tomb was empty. Two of them were on their way to Emmaus. While they talked with each other about all these things that had happened, the resurrected Jesus came to them and talked with them. After that event, they ran into Jerusalem, where Jesus' disciples were gathered. And they told the disciples about meeting the resurrected Jesus. The disciples couldn't believe the story was true. Imagine how the disciples must have felt when they were together in Jerusalem, after watching their Master helplessly die on the cross. Before he was crucified, they spent significant time with Jesus. They had walked proudly by the crowd who were trying to touch and talk to Jesus. They witnessed with their eyes that people's lives were changed once they encountered Jesus. They would have thought that they could do anything if they were with Jesus. Having experienced Jesus' power, some of them expected Jesus to be a king, a political king for them.

Later, it turns to a totally different story. Their master was dead. Even worse, he was crucified, which was considered most disgraceful. How could Jesus die in such a shameful way! They ran away from Roman soldiers, denying that they knew Jesus. They were sitting around with sadness, despair, and fear. They totally forgot the word that Jesus left them, which John recorded: "I will not leave you as orphans; I will come to you" (John 14:18, NIV).

Preoccupied with sadness and despair, they couldn't believe the news that Jesus was alive! It was no wonder they didn't recognize the resurrected Jesus standing before them. Jesus started the conversation with a greeting: "Peace be with you." They were startled and terrified. They thought that it must be a ghost! The resurrected Jesus showed his hands and feet to them, and let them touch the scars where he was nailed. While the disciples were still wondering and doubting, Jesus asked for food to eat. They gave him a piece of broiled fish; Jesus took it and ate in their presence. Then the disciples recognized the resurrected Jesus. The news that Jesus was alive became real to them. Their spiritual eyes were opened.

After their eyes were opened, Jesus taught them that all the promises revealed in the Old Testament were fulfilled. The disciples finally understood why Jesus had to die on the cross and rise from death. Now they became a different people. They were not who they used to be. While Jesus was with his disciples, he had talked continuously about his death and resurrection. However, they did not understand what he really meant or the purpose of Jesus' ministry. They knew about Jesus and his ministry, but they did not know him in a true sense. But now, after meeting the resurrected Jesus, they realized Jesus Christ had to die and rise from death so that all people and all nations would be saved.

When they had been convinced of Jesus' crucifixion and resurrection, Jesus commanded them to be witnesses of all that happened. He commanded them to proclaim repentance and forgiveness of sins to all nations. Then, he asked them to stay in the city, Jerusalem, until they received the promise from God. If we look into the first chapter of the book of Acts, we can easily recognize that the promise of God comes as the Holy Spirit.

Here I wondered why Jesus commanded his followers to stay in Jerusalem rather than immediately sending them out to spread the kingdom of God. Jesus didn't ask them to receive the power right away. He asked them to stay in the city, Jerusalem. Jerusalem was the place where there was sadness from losing their teacher. Jerusalem was the place they experienced despair and lost hope in their future. Jerusalem was the place where there was fear: they were afraid that people who were against Jesus Christ would chase after them. Jerusalem was the place where there were guilty feelings for denying Jesus.

But Jerusalem was also the place of the temple, the place to worship. Therefore, Jerusalem was the place of human brokenness and at the same time, a place of worship full of the Holy Spirit's power. Stay in the city where sadness and temple coexist; in other words, Jesus asked them to worship with their broken hearts. Worship with our broken hearts.

Speaking of broken hearts, we tend to think of this state of heart as the thing we should run away from, the thing we need to overcome. Rather, a broken heart is the point where you begin your worship of God, because it brings desire for something to heal. A broken heart brings desperation for something more. Broken hearts prepare us to be responsive to the Word of God. After his adultery with Bathsheba and with a broken heart, David sang, "The sacrifice acceptable to God is a broken spirit; a broken and contrite heart, O God, you will not despise" (Psalm 51:17, NRSV). As a hungry child seeks for her mother to give her things to eat, so a broken person looks for God to show her God's presence. Of course, God is everywhere. But when we seek God's face with desperation, God turns God's face to us.

With mixed feelings of sadness, despair, guilt, and confusion, the disciples met the resurrected Jesus and became desperate for the promise of God to be fulfilled. Into such a state of their hearts, the power of the Holy Spirit came. All confusion and doubts were gone. They bore witness to Jesus Christ, and their lives became a powerful history, as the Acts of the Apostles relates.

I think that one of the enemies of a Christian life is complacency. We might say that we have a good program, enough people to worship, a good ministry, enough money, a happy life, faith in God, belief in Jesus' death and resurrection. It is good that God has blessed us that much. But if we want to receive the power like the disciples did, things won't be enough to get ready to be a witness, for our lives to affect others.

This morning, the Scripture challenges us to maintain the lifestyle of brokenness, to be desperate for God. When we keep seeking God's face with a broken heart and worship God, the presence of God will be with us. Once the power of God comes upon us, we will be a powerful witness and affect others' lives. Just as Jesus healed one woman's hemorrhage by her touching the fringe of his clothes, we will know God.

Jesus asks us to have true faith in his death and resurrection. And to stand up from a satisfactory place to affect other lives. Worship God with our brokenness. Be desperate for God. Let us surrender our lives to a broken heart that will bring revival, first in us and then in the city. Amen.

A version of this sermon was preached on July, 23, 2006, at Francis Asbury United Methodist Church, Rockville, Maryland.

22

God Specializes in Comebacks

Lisa M. Tait

JOHN 11:1-44

Jesus said to her, "Your brother will rise again." (John 11:23, NIV)

Recently my husband and I had the pleasure of viewing one of the greatest tennis matches of all time. We stumbled on it by accident one lazy Saturday afternoon. This match was considered phenomenal by commentators and viewers alike because the challenger, Serena Williams, was ranked number 81, and she was playing the number-one-seeded player in the world. It was the final match of the 2007 Australian Open. Serena demolished Maria Sharapova. Serena dominated play. We couldn't help but focus on the intensity on her face. She was unwavering, determined, her body perfectly chiseled. She looked like someone who knew she was destined to leave a champion.

The sixty-three-minute match was incredible to watch. But the story behind Serena's journey to that winner's circle was most astonishing. In the previous year, Serena was plagued with a knee injury that sidelined her. She played only sixteen matches in 2006 and slumped as low as number 140 in the rankings. Most people had written her off, and it was as if the Williams sisters' reign had died. Serena's career seemingly had died, but now she stood on the platform holding the trophy and thanking God in her acceptance speech.

In our focal Scripture, Lazarus, the brother of Mary and Martha, has fallen ill, and his illness turns fatal. Death has beaten Lazarus, and he has been counted out. This story of healing and resurrection by

106

Christ is so compelling because it is so personal. Many people Jesus healed or resurrected were complete strangers. But not Lazarus; Lazarus was a brother beloved. Mary and Martha, followers of Christ, had witnessed Jesus' power to heal the sick for themselves. So they sent word for Jesus to come to Bethany and heal their brother. Jesus delayed his trip to Bethany and, by the time he arrived, Lazarus had been dead and buried four days.

I want to take a fresh look at Lazarus's story and see if it can help breathe new life into someone's dead situation today. This text teaches that we will all experience some debilitating devastation in our lives, a prolonged defeat or distress that seems to have no end. How can we enjoy sunshine if we never experience rain? How do we recognize plenty if we never wallow in want? The truth is that we all experience trials, heartbreak, and betrayal. As Christians, we want to believe we are somehow safeguarded against calamity. But the reality is, God "sends rain on the righteous and the unrighteous" (Matthew 5:45, NIV), and bad things really do happen to good people!

In other words, we are not alone in our experience of pain and suffering. Every human encounters situations that move from bad to worse. In Serena Williams's case, during her hiatus from tennis, she was plagued with a knee injury. And she struggled with overwhelming grief because of the random murder of her sister, Yetunde. Things went from bad to worse. In the first verse of John 11, John records, "Now a man named Lazarus was sick." But thirteen verses later, Lazarus's situation moves from bad to worse and Jesus tells the disciples plainly, "Lazarus is dead." Things went from bad to worse.

Some scholars suggest Jesus recognized this sickness would bring glory to God and to his Son. But this glory would be achieved only if Lazarus actually died. So Jesus stayed where he was for two days after receiving the message. While it may seem as though all hope is lost as time passes, this text teaches us that a delay is not a denial. It teaches us that help is on the way. No matter how bad our situation, it's not over until God gets the glory!

Jesus' well-thought-out delay was nothing more than a setup for God's miraculous glory to unfold. To fully embrace this reality, we must understand that according to rabbinical tradition, the soul hovers by the grave for three days hoping to reunite with the body, but at the first sign of decomposition (the fourth day), it departs finally.[1] Jesus is trying to get us to see that our prolonged pain, our seemingly irresolvable situation, is nothing more than the prelude God requires to perform a comeback.

In Lazarus's case, his sickness turned to death. In our case, it might be that our bills turn to bankruptcy; those disagreements turn to divorce, our child's pranks turn to juvenile prison; that cough turns to cancer; problems at work turn to unemployment. But we must know that this will not end in death; know that "all things work together for good to them that love God" (Romans 8:28, KJV). Know that it's not over until God says it's over! Remember this: God will not give the final benediction over your situation until God gets the glory!

Another lesson this text teaches us is that in order for us to experience a comeback, there must be a revelation. The devastation occurs. Lazarus is dead. Martha receives word that Jesus is coming, so she goes to meet him, saying, "Lord, if you had been here, my brother would not have died, but I know that even now God will give you whatever you ask" (John 11:21, NIV). Martha's faith causes her to make a resounding revelation. She has full confidence in the efficacy of Jesus' power, his influence with God, and the sincerity of his friendship. She believes Jesus can stand between her brother and death. She allows the lowest moment in her life to strengthen her faith. Her faith was really in a storm. The night was dark, and there was no light but that of the resurrection; but that light was too dim and distant to provide support.

If the truth were told, many of us are experiencing our own faith storms. We wonder if there is any light at the end of this tunnel. But I am convinced that our greatest revelations come in our devastation. In John 11:25, Christ reveals himself as the resurrection and the life. Martha's faith has been tested to its limits, and she realizes that no matter how bad things look, she is standing before the one power who is able to provide an "even now" blessing.

This is the revelation God invites us to encounter: no matter how hopeless and dead our situations may appear, Jesus is the resurrection and the life. It is our job to speak to life's situation and proclaim "even now" that God can move in this situation. It may require us to repeat it every day, to speak it even in the absence of evidence, but once we embrace this revelation, it has the power to change our world.

We must have faith in God's "even now" ability. Like Serena Williams, we must allow the past to remain in the past and trust God to make a comeback through us. When Serena dropped in the rankings from number 1 in the world to number 141, I'm sure she thought about hanging up that racket and throwing in the towel. She had earned enough money, and certainly she had left a legacy in tennis. But like Martha, she knew there was still some life in the situation. There was still some hope, some expectation, some belief that her career wasn't over and that "even now" God could perform a comeback in her life. There will be some devastation in our lives, but recognize that it is the ideal time to receive a revelation.

A final lesson in this text I want to lift up is that there must be a proclamation. In the postlude to this devastation, Jesus makes a powerful proclamation in at least three areas. He makes a personal proclamation directly to Martha, who shares with Jesus how bad the situation seems: "But, Lord, by this time there is a bad odor, for he has been there four days" (John 11:39, NIV). Jesus pushes Martha to practice her faith. He says, "Did I not tell you that if you believed, you would see the glory of God?" (v. 40, NIV). We all are confronted by this personal proclamation. We must decide to believe that Jesus truly is the Resurrection and the Life, and that no situation is beyond the saving grace of God.

Then Jesus makes a public proclamation. In verse 42, Jesus begins a conversation with his heavenly Father. He pauses, however, to address those who are grieving, because he ultimately wants them to believe in God. He wanted Lazarus's resurrection to show the crowd that he was sent from the Father. They had heard Jesus' words; now they needed to believe in him.

Our deliverance is bigger than us. When God performs a comeback in our lives, it is so the entire community may be blessed and believe. There must be a personal proclamation in our lives so that we will activate our faith. There must also be a public proclamation so people around us who see our dilemma will come to know that no problem is too great for God.

Then Jesus makes a prophetic proclamation. Jesus shares with his disciples that Lazarus's illness would not lead to death, but instead it would be for God's glory. In this final proclamation, Jesus calls out in a loud voice, "Lazarus, come out!" This prophetic proclamation affirms all Jesus spoke earlier. Lazarus's condition did not end with death, and our situations also will not end with death.

The prophetic proclamation declares that our situations are not beyond God. There is no need for us to throw in the towel or give up hope. Our Creator proclaims a resurrection in our situations. Even now God is speaking to the dead places in our lives and proclaiming that we will live again, we will love again, we will prosper again, we will rejoice again, we will be healthy again, and our families will come back together again. Jesus said, "Lazarus, come out!" and from what was dead, God brings forth life.

Whenever storms rage in our lives, we must remember that God gave us Jesus as the example of the greatest comeback the world has ever seen. When the world had turned its back on the Savior, when people had mocked and scorned him, when they whipped him all night long, when they cast lots for his clothes, when they marched him up Golgotha's hill, when they placed nails in his feet and hands and a crown of thorns upon his head, when they pierced him in his side, we witnessed the greatest devastation known to humanity. But I'm so glad the story didn't end there. A prophetic proclamation had already been made, and on the third day he rose again, with all power in his hands.

If Serena can come back, if Lazarus can come back, and if Jesus can come back, we too can come back. After we have experienced some debilitating devastation, after we have received a resounding revelation, after we have embraced his powerful proclamation, I believe it's time for some serious celebration.

Celebrate that we're coming back with more power. Celebrate that we're coming back with greater wisdom. Celebrate that we're coming back with an unwavering faith, and we're coming back with a greater testimony. God specializes in comebacks, and your victory is already sealed. Hallelujah!

A version of this sermon was preached at Liberty Temple Baptist Church, Detroit, Michigan, on February 18, 2007, and at Imani Christian Center, Stone Mountain, Georgia, on May 6, 2007.

1. George Buttrick, *The Interpreter's Bible* (Nashville: Abingdon, 1952), 642.

23

The Fullness of Resurrection[1]

Anne-Marie Jeffery

JOHN 11:21-27
Martha said to Jesus, "Lord, if you had been here, my brother would not have died." (John 11:21, NRSV)

My sisters and brothers, we have a tendency not to believe in the fullness of Jesus' resurrection. We doubt the presence of our Savior in times of grief because this gift is so amazing that we can barely wrap our minds around it. We have been given a powerful blessing that is beyond our finite minds to comprehend—so much so that we let this blessing go by without truly grasping what it is, especially when we lose a loved one. Beloved, in sorrowful times, when we are presented with this divine grace, we can miss the promise that our Lord has bestowed upon us. Our almighty God sent his Son that we might be raised; and, yet, in many forms and fashions, so we say, like Martha in the Gospel, "Lord, if you had been here, our loved one, Anetha, would not have died," because our present pain keeps us from what we know to be true.

Today we have come to celebrate the life of Anetha Hollingsworth—a believer, a "born Anglican." We come together in our grief and in our thankfulness for who she was. I first met Anetha Hollingsworth when I was a very new priest. James, her son, a member of our congregation at Epiphany, asked me if I could bring his mother communion. Now, I am from the West Indies, as are Anetha and her family, and I know the importance of home communion for West Indians. I am not saying it

111

is not important for Americans; but for West Indians, when they cannot get to church, home communion is extremely important.

So I went out to see her with communion kit in hand—and just a bit of nervousness. I had never met her. She was almost one hundred years old at the time. I wondered what she would think of this new priest—a woman—representing a change in Anglican doctrine that I'm certain she did not grow up with. I came into the house and was welcomed in and led to her bedroom. There I met a most amazing lady, who welcomed me with joy and hospitality. I remember that even that first time I met her she had such light about her. She listened to who I was and welcomed me. We talked and prayed, and I gave her and other family members communion. She was glad to know that I, too, was West Indian; and I was delighted to hear that she was a "born Anglican." She told me the names of the churches in Guyana in which she had been baptized and confirmed, and I was sad to tell her that I did not know the priests she mentioned from that time. But I remember leaving with a sense of lightness, a sense of happiness, and a sense of joy. Anetha Hollingsworth had many gifts to give.

A few months later, I attended her hundredth birthday party and left with some great West Indian food. Over the next few years, I visited her now and again—though not as often as I would have liked. Busy schedules got in the way. But each time I came, she welcomed me. Each time, she was so happy to receive communion—the body and blood of Christ—and each time, I left with a sense of joy. I am thankful that I visited her a few weeks ago and found the same joyous person who always declared she was a "born Anglican." The name Anglican has conflicting connotations right now. You may have heard a lot on the news about the discord between the Anglican Communion and the Episcopal Church. In all that, it is easy to forget what most Anglicans, and Episcopalians, are: worshipers of God, lovers of God, people who are committed to their faith, believers in Jesus Christ. When Anetha Hollingsworth declared that she was a "born Anglican," she was talking about the faith she had been steeped in, about her love of her Lord and Savior Jesus Christ, and about coming to the Table to receive his body and blood to be renewed. Anetha had a deep faith. She knew that God was very good and that God was an essential part of her life.

In our Gospel reading, when Jesus first shows up after Lazarus's death, Martha greets him by saying, "Lord, if you had been here, my brother would not have died." Jesus reassures her, saying, "He will rise again." Martha agrees. She responds with a sentence that reflects a common belief among Jews about resurrection at the time: "I know that he will rise again in the resurrection on the last day" (John 11:24, NRSV). But Jesus goes further. He says, "I am the resurrection and the life. Those who believe in me, even though they die, will live, and everyone who lives and believes in me will never die" (vv. 25-26, NRSV).

Now, Martha is a believer. She is a believer in Jesus, and she is his friend. She does not need to be told to believe. She knows that one day her brother will be raised. And yet she has worries and doubts. Jesus answers her by going deeper. He tells her, "I am the resurrection and the life. I can raise your brother up now—not only at the end of time." And Martha responds, "Yes, Lord, I believe that you are the Messiah, the Son of God, the one coming into the world" (v. 27, NRSV).

Jesus is the Messiah, and he has come into this world. He has died on the cross, has been raised up, and raises us up—if we are willing, if we are ready, if we are ready to believe in his power. Jesus tells us that physical death has no power over us because he is the Resurrection and the Life. These are mighty words, which is why we started this worship service with them. These are such powerful words that we can barely take them in. This gift of resurrection is so wondrous that we can hardly grasp its meaning; yet often we let these words go past us, not letting ourselves enter into the immensity of God's gift. When we lose a loved one, we are confronted with the question of resurrection. In our grief, it is difficult to take in just how much Jesus is giving us. We are like larva in water that cannot comprehend that one day they will be dragonflies and fly around in the air. How can we take in the meaning of the resurrection? How can we go from the place where we say, "Lord, why weren't you here when we needed you?" to the one where we declare, "You are the Resurrection, the Messiah, the Son of God in the world who is with us always"?

Jesus tells us to believe. He invites us to believe. He doesn't say how much or how little to believe. He doesn't say how much faith we are to have. Jesus says, "Believe." We just have to take that step, daring to believe that we will live even though we die, daring to believe that Jesus is the Messiah who has come and is still coming into the world.

Anetha believed. You could see it in every part of her. She took joy in Jesus. She loved the Lord, and we know God has raised her up. She is no longer with us, and that is hard. We knew we could not keep her always, and we take comfort that she is with God. This does not mean we will not grieve her passing. But as we grieve, we are reminded of Jesus' daring promise to all of us: "I am the resurrection and the life. Whoever has faith in me shall have life." So as we celebrate Anetha Josephine Hollingsworth, a believer in Jesus, cling to your love of God, to your love of Christ, and to your belief that God will not let death conquer us. Hold on to the promise that Jesus will take care of us and raise us up. Take that step to knowing that Jesus is the Messiah, the Son of God, who is coming right now into this world.

This sermon was preached May 5, 2007, at St. John's Episcopal Church in Mount Rainer, Maryland, at the funeral of Anetha Hollingsworth, 102 years old at the time of her death. Originally from Guyana, West Indies, Ms. Hollingsworth lived most of her life in the United States.

1. I owe many thanks to my small group at The Festival of Women of Color Preachers, April 2007, led by Dr. Katie G. Cannon and Dr. Ella P. Mitchell. They and three other great women preachers got this sermon started and gave me a new confidence in my preaching.

24

Three Moons in My Moccasins

Holly Haile Davis

JOHN 12:20-33

"Whoever serves me must follow me, and where I am, there will my servant be also." (John 12:26, NRSV)

I have European ancestors, I have African ancestors, and mostly I have Shinnecock ancestors. I am a Shinnecock Indian. A little old federal judge told me so.[1] Yet the Shinnecock Hills, the circling hawk, the Shinnecock Bay, the Mecox Bay, and Arabash Creek had already told me that I am a Shinnecock Indian. And the air at PowWow time and the wood smoke and the chill in early September, and the peaceful and blessed sunset at the reservation cemetery long ago told us, and tells me now, who I am, and together declared this truth that "this is the land of the Shinnecock" and "we are the people of the meadows by the shore, we are *the* people of this land." It was to peasants, "the people of the land," that Jesus came with Good News.

"Sir, we wish to see Jesus," requested some Greeks who were outside the disciples' in crowd. Red Jacket, a Seneca Indian, said the same thing. One of the Iroquois' greatest orators, Red Jacket's fiery, insightful eloquence inspired cultural pride and resistance among his Indian people and sometimes affected the behavior of his non-Indian hearers. He understood English but determinedly refused to speak it in public. Red Jacket, in response to the missionary Cram, said among other things regarding Cram's attempt to convert the Seneca people in 1805:

Brother, we have been told that you have been preaching to the white people in this place. . . . We will wait a little while and see what effect your preaching has upon them. If we find it does them good, makes them honest and less disposed to cheat Indians, we will consider again what you have said. . . . But for now, walk for a while—and maybe we will see if the journey through life in *your* moccasins is indeed a *Canku Wasté,* a Good Road of Life.[2]

In these weeks of Lent, we move closer to the hour, the hour from which we dare not ask to be removed; because we have said we wish to follow; that where this Jesus leads, we may be also, making sure not to love our lives and the trappings of our lives more than we love our desire to follow Jesus. And which way does he go?

Jesus shows that his life and the life of discipleship is a contradiction to the normalcy of civilization's systems of rule, control, and dominance. His is a continual call for justice.[3] In this world, domination systems are characterized by political oppression, that is, the many being ruled by the few powerful, wealthy, elite; domination systems are social structures characterized by economic exploitation in that most of society's wealth stays in the hands of and is paid to the wealthy. And domination systems enjoy what Marcus Borg and John Dominic Crossan call "religious legitimation," that is, the social order reflects the will of God.

As Jesus walks his ministry through Lent, through Holy Week he talks about the kind of death he will die while at the same time teaching about what kind of life disciples shall live if they choose to actually follow him. To put it another way,

Justice has to do, not with a "proper believing," or a "creedal orthodoxy," but with how well or how poorly each nation, and by implication each person within that nation, perceives the "face of the Divine" in the faces of the hungry, thirsty, the stranger, the naked, the sick, the dispossessed and the imprisoned.[4]

Not far from this spot in 1876, the *Circassian* shipwrecked, and along with local white men, ten Shinnecock Indians perished. We are children of the widows and orphans of the *Circassian*. We are among those who continue to seek justice, even as justice continues to elude us. Not far from this spot in 2006, families with very modest houses face, not an outpouring of concern for justice in this wealthiest of communities in the whole wide world today, but losing their homes. There are reports that real-estate-hungry folk try to get these people to sell their houses by calling, by knocking on doors and windows, and by hitting and pounding on exterior walls late in the night. Let me be very clear about this: the home owners whose walls are being beaten on in the middle of the night are African American families while affluent newcomers with an insatiable appetite for mini and mega Hamptons mansions are white.

The median annual income in the United States is $40,000; the same source reported the official poverty level in this nation for a household of four in the 1990s was $18,104.[5] Another source reported that in order for a household of one to be eligible to apply for low/moderate income units in Southampton town, their income cannot exceed $49,750; and for a family of four, their income must not exceed $71,000 in order to be eligible for low/moderate income housing units here in the town of Southampton.[6] But the average household income for residents on the Shinnecock Indian Reservation by the 2000 census is $14,000 a year.[7] A person working full-time at $10 an hour produces an annual income of about $20,000; and working at the average national minimum wage produces a whopping $11,000.

I believe one of the most important questions in our global community today is: Do nations have the right to do within their own borders what they wish? Native American nations have the right to exist. I can say that, but do we? It is a theological question; it is also a political question, an economic question, an educational, social, medical, and quality-of-life question. If we decide that we do have the right to exist, we will have to come to that conclusion because of what we believe about life and because of what we believe about God.

While attending a lecture at the National Cathedral College for Preachers in Washington, D.C., I met a Presbyterian elder from Greensboro, North Carolina. She shared with me an experience she'd had. This elder, Mary-Ellen, is white and is both a professional Christian educator in the Presbyterian church and a teacher in a Greensboro school. Her colleagues in their local school consisted of an entirely white teaching staff, except for one black woman whom I will call Annie. Annie did not allow others to exploit her and use her as the resident, one-size-fits-all, past, present, and future expert on all things African American. Tensions mounted among the staff days before mandatory diversity training, as white teachers grumbled and groused. By the time they were at table together, folks were edgy; the mood was unpleasant. When the white teachers finally voiced their objections to this program, Annie was moved to speak. She told her coworkers stories about growing up with "white only" and "colored" bathrooms and fountains. The most upsetting thing about this story, I believe, is that Annie had hundreds of stories like this; and just as upsetting is the fact that there are families represented in this congregation today who have not one story like this but hundreds.

Diversity is more than a Johnny-come-very-lately politically correct policy; diversity is more than a minority minute to be politely observed or endured before the real business starts or after the important business is concluded; diversity is more than many differently tinted faces decorating our scenery, creating colorful photo ops. Diversity allows us to see Jesus.

Though the church purports to see Jesus, alleges to know God, claims to be about doing justice, loving kindness, and walking humbly with God, it is not what I have observed. My own take on Jesus' understanding of the prophets is that divine worship doesn't excuse the church from seeking divine justice. The Jesus I see stands with prophets against temple worship that, rather than empowering justice, excuses folks from it; and in that, I see a Jesus who also stands against forms of Christianity used for centuries to support imperial violence and injustice.

Three moons in my moccasins will reveal to you that the state of New York and the township of Southampton and, now, the Gristedes millionaires have joined the howling pack of those who challenge the Shinnecock Nation's right to exist. We have been hauled into federal court; we have been maligned and smeared in the media; we have survived in our ancestral lands not because of the grace of our neighbors and their churches and not because of the kindness of the officials. And yet basic human dignity issues such as substandard, unsafe housing continue to plague our community. Employment opportunities we've attempted to create have been thwarted, and now there are wealth and power behind efforts to take away the small industry with which we as Indian people feed 10 percent of our own population. Those of us affiliated with Presbyterian churches of the Presbytery of Long Island are in communion and in community with the powers that be who support and benefit from policies and practices that thrive on continuing political oppression, economic exploitation, and religious legitimatization, and feed the system that dominates and brings violence to our lives.

A young Guatemalan woman said a few months before she was killed by the military, "What good is life unless you give it away— unless you can give it for a better world, even if you never see that world but have only carried your grain of sand to the building site. Then you're fulfilled as a person."[8] Among the Onondoga people it is said, "What you give away, you get." I believe that, just as I believe it was Jesus' passion that got him killed, and I believe also that he knowingly walked his *Canku Wasté*, his Good Road, anyhow.

Today we will remember and give thanks for the gifts of those who were leaders among us and who have died during the last year. And as we also prepare to share a meal in the tradition of Indian people of this land, I would like us to remember this image: we are here to share gifts from God, to divide up the life we live (some life over here, a little life over there), the food we aportion. We have enough. God has provided enough as it passes through the hands of the One whose path we follow, each in our own moccasins, for he is, and we can be, the incarnation of divine justice. May we not be afraid to actively seek justice, for we are children of the God of life; we are children of the God of justice. A-hau. Amen.

Let us pray: Great Spirit, grant that I may not judge my siblings until I have walked for three moons in their moccasins. Amen.

A longer version of this sermon was preached on March 28, 2007, at the Bridgehampton Presbyterian Church for the Long Island Presbytery meeting Tabutne`.

1. Judge Thomas C. Platt, U.S.D.J., Case 2:03-cv03243-TCP-ARL, Endnote #7, "Shinnecock Indian Nation (the Shinnecock Tribe) is an Indian tribe."

2. Bob Blaisdell, ed., *Great Speeches by Native Americans* (New York: Dover, 2000), 41ff.

3. Marcus J. Borg and John Dominic Crossan, *The Last Week: The Day-by-Day Account of Jesus' Final Week in Jerusalem* (New York: HarperCollins, 2006), 74.

4. John Shelby Spong, *The Sins of Scripture* (New York: HarperSanFrancisco, 2005), 163.

5. Marcus J. Borg, "Bringing the Vision to Congregations: Spirituality and Personal Transformation" packet (2006), 5, 7.

6. Cover Letter, John C. White, Director of Housing, Town of Southampton Housing Office, Application Packet, Southampton, NY, November 10, 2005.

7. Tom Durante, "The Waiting Game," *Long Island Press*, New York (January 12, 2006), 9.

8. Jim Wallis, "Faithful to the Truth," *Sojourners* 18, no. 2 (December 4, 1989): 5.

25

Behold! From the Other Side of Resurrection

Dionne P. Boissière

JOHN 19:26-27

When Jesus saw his mother and the disciple whom he loved standing beside her, he said to his mother, "Woman, here is your son." Then he said to the disciple, "Here is your mother." And from that hour the disciple took her into his own home. (John 19:26-27, NRSV)

In the seven last words or phrases of Christ, we become onlookers of this crucifixion event as the divine descendants of Abraham and Sarah, Isaac and Rebekah, and Jacob, Leah, and Rachel. We are engrafted branches. We are inheritors of God's grace and mercy. As we experience Jesus' words from the cross, we can no longer deny who we are. Christ speaks to us today. We have this life-giving text that records the story in which the Gospel writers have so wonderfully described the passion of our beloved Christ.

We not only have this documented narrative from which we are charged to preach and teach, but in this day, we who can speak from the other side of resurrection are able to look death in the face and see the promise of new life in Christ. We now have the hope of salvation and have been given the ministry of reconciliation. We know that Christ's resurrection did come, and because of it we experience the power of God's Holy Spirit. For without death we never could have known what it means to have access to the ultimate power source.

From the other side of resurrection, we see many injustices of a dying world. It is not enough to be onlookers of the crucifixion. We can never again read through the passion of Christ and the moments leading to Jesus' death as though it were a story meant for us to recount year after year as just an exercise of reflection and solemn memorial. If we say we are Christ's disciples today, we must, then, deny ourselves, pick up our own crosses, and sometimes those of our sisters and brothers, daily and follow the example of Jesus the Christ. From the other side of resurrection, we have no other choice but to echo the words of the apostles Peter and John and say to the church and to humanity, "We cannot keep from speaking about what we have seen and heard" (Acts 4:20, NRSV). We, who are on the other side of the resurrection, have a panoramic view, the whole picture. We not only have the words of God captured in the text to give us hope, but also we have our actual encounter with the sovereign God through the person of Jesus the Christ, empowered by God's Holy Spirit, which allows us to speak of this great passion story from a different place.

As we look deeper into these few verses, this third word Jesus speaks from the cross proves God is speaking still! As the NRSV translates, "Woman, *here* is your son!" Then to the disciple, "*Here* is your mother" God still is speaking to all disciples and to all of God's beloved creation right now! Have we listened? Just as Jesus, while in pain and anguish, dying a slow and torturous death, has a word of love, a word of comfort, and makes provision for his mother from the cross, so Jesus is calling out to us even now, saying, "Behold!"

Jesus speaks only twice from the cross to humanity. The first time is found in Luke's Gospel account when Jesus speaks to the thief on his right side assuring him of a place beside him in paradise (Luke 23:43). From the other side of resurrection, we hear Jesus speak now and see this thief as a symbol of humanity—frail, guilty, marginalized, ostracized, disenfranchised, and hurting. Yet even in this marred condition, Jesus responds to him, to us, with sincere love and compassion so that redemption can come. Here in John's Gospel, Jesus speaks and addresses his mother and the beloved disciple. Jesus calls out to his mother, but he doesn't cry, "Mother." Jesus specifically says, "Woman." The Greek word used here refers to a woman of any age. Jesus is also very specific when he speaks to the disciple. The Greek word used is the word for "a son." Jesus is making provisions for his mother and his followers, charging them even in his dying moments to take care of each other. Jesus' words not only resounded from the cross centuries ago, but resound even right now!

Jesus' words are meant to speak to humanity and say, "Behold! Here am I!" The very word "behold" means to see, to view, observe, to watch closely, to consider or regard. It is the active present tense. It is no accident that Jesus speaks to his mother. It is no accident that Christ speaks to the one who is his beloved friend and brother. Jesus redeems him, just as he did the thief on his right and tells this beloved disciple, "Behold your mother." And so Jesus says to humanity now, to outcasts, nonconformists, the fearful, the mocked, the weak, the guilty, and the broken, to all of creation, "Behold!" Look first at me, and then behold all these things.

Behold our children and our children's children being left behind, abused, and feeling ashamed of who they are. Behold the powers and principalities, wickedness in high places. Behold the horrors of war, rumors of war, and the byproduct of greed, human genocide. Behold the ruin and utter devastation left by Hurricane Katrina and the havoc of its aftermath along the Gulf Coast. Behold the tsunamis, earthquakes, tornadoes, and other natural disasters ravaging our beloved planet. Behold the lie of putting religion over relationship with God who loved the world and brought the hope of eternal and abundant life to all. Behold the divisiveness and dissension entrenched within Christian religious denominations. Behold the illnesses killing humanity: childhood obesity, depression, over- and under-the-counter drugs, hypertension, cancer, AIDS, and diabetes. Behold the face of racism, sexism, ageism, classism, and negative *-isms* and discriminations of all kinds. Behold broken relationships due to broken promises, broken hearts, and broken dreams all as a result of a broken people. Behold our brothers and sisters in Africa, South America, and all our countries of origin and even around the corner, who are hungry, homeless, refugees, POWs, ignored, manipulated, prostituted, and left feeling unloved. Behold death. Look at it, look at me, not from any other place, but from this place, our place as children from the other side of resurrection. We know all too well that in order for us to have life, we must experience death; this is the paradox of our faith, that life comes out of death and death precedes life. We cannot have the hope of Resurrection Sunday without the pain of Good Friday. We must behold the realities of death that exist in our lives in all its forms and comprehend its meaning for our future. Because we have the view from the other side of resurrection, however, we cannot merely observe, but we must heed Jesus' divine imperative to behold and take action!

If we look at the final verse of our text, it says, "From that hour the disciple took her into his own home." We see that Jesus' imperative was not simply a call for two persons to take a moment and look at one another in their present state of grief, but it was a holy mandate to "behold," triggering an individual and communal response and sounding off an urgent call to action! We are the prophets now standing at the foot of our own crosses and cannot be afraid to look at the hell in our lives and the hell in the lives of our sisters and brothers. And seeing, we must respond to their situation! From the other side of resurrection, we cannot simply be mouthpieces for God, but we must be true agents of God's grace and conduits of God's mercy, compassion, and justice. If we simply look at humanity in its corrupt state and do nothing, then we mock the redemptive act of Christ Jesus. If we look at the fact that African Americans accounted for 49 percent of the 42,514 estimated AIDS cases diagnosed in the United States[1] and we do nothing, then we crucify Jesus all over again. If we simply look at the 132.7 million orphans worldwide or the 12 million children in sub-Saharan Africa who no longer have parents due to the AIDS epidemic[2] or the 7.8 million people living with HIV in South and Southeast Asia[3] and we do nothing, then we crucify Jesus all over again.

How can we hear the words of Jesus newly spoken to us year after year and continue to be sideline servants of the Most High God? We ought to behold all these things from the other side of resurrection and do as Jesus told the beloved disciple to do. Bring those who are hurting, sick, dying, orphaned, or widowed, those who are grieving, misunderstood, and oppressed into our lives! Take the seriousness of their plight into our own dwelling places, literally and spiritually, and work toward complete deliverance and demand justice. We who stand on the other side of the resurrection, the ones who claim to overcome by the blood of the Lamb and the word of our testimony. Behold from a place of victory in Christ Jesus! Look and see all of it for who and what we are and love as Christ loved. Let us speak the promises of God we know to be true and that we believe will bring healing, restoration, hope, and reconciliation to all God's creation. And then move from a glance to extend a hand and offer a place in God that brings the hope and courage to behold a world from the other side of resurrection. Amen.

A version of this sermon was preached during a "Jesus' Seven Last Words from the Cross" program on April 14, 2006, at First Reformed Church of Jamaica, Queens, New York.

1. "HIV Statistics: HIV/AIDS among African Americans," http://www.aboutaids.com/ (accessed February 2006).

2. "AIDS and Orphans," www.worldvision.org (accessed January 2006).

3. UNAIDS—World Health Organization: Global Facts and Figures—Regional Statistics, 2006.

26
It Is Finished

Valerie Bridgeman Davis

JOHN 19:30

When Jesus had received the wine, he said, "It is finished." Then he bowed his head and gave up his spirit. (John 19:30, NRSV)

I am a basketball fan. So college basketball's pinnacle event, March Madness, always captures my imagination. I look for the underdog story or the overcoming-all-odds story. I watch for the one-that-got-away story, or the rare who-would-have-believed-it story.

This year, the story came in the form of the University of Florida Gators team. I must confess, in the spirit of full disclosure, that I am a Texas Longhorns fan. I wanted to see Kevin Durant succeed as a classy and classic wunderkind freshman. But that wasn't the story this time. This time the story belongs to five young men of the Florida team—five young men who returned after winning last year to win again. They became the first team to go back to back since Duke in 1992 and the first ever to repeat with the same starting five players. Their coach, Billy Donovan, said about them, "I think this team should go down as one of the best teams in college basketball history; not as the most talented, and not on style points—but because they encompassed what the word 'team' means."[1] It was a rarity: guys who didn't jump for the big league and the big money, guys who risked losing and being seen as foolish for finishing what they started. A rarity: seeing it to the end, even when they didn't know what the end would be.

I'm still not a University of Florida fan. But I am a fan of five guys with heart, especially Joakim Noah, who was called the heart of that team. I'm a fan of finishing, of running on to see what the end will be. I'm a fan of the final four, of the one shining, glorious moment that lingers in the air, of that famous championship question: "What are you going to do next?"

The Johannine community also must have been fans of the final moment. Here in the Gospel story are the last recorded words of Jesus, just before he hung his head and died: "It is finished." Task completed. Scratch that off. Knowing that all was fulfilled, having agonized for this coming moment, having endured the doubts of disciples and the disdain of dissenters, now, in this final moment, resolve takes hold of the beaten brow and the bruised head.

The truth is, the disciples were in dismay and discouraged. They had hoped he would redeem Israel; at least that's what the travelers to Emmaus would later say to the Resurrected One. But here, in that final moment, there is no shine. There is no glory that they can see. All they can see is death: the death of their hopes, the death of their teacher, the death of their visions. And they hear the voice of the One they've listened to for years, months, days, hours: "It is finished."

What? What is finished? It's done? How will they go on if it's over? What is accomplished, they would want to know. And the truth is that is our question still. In the moments leading to the silence of the grave, the days before resurrection, what gets accomplished? How do we live into the unknown?

I don't know about you, but I've been at the end of one task, staring into the silence of the between time: the "that's-done-what's-next" time. And I've often been more doubting disciple than confident Christ. It's done, but what's next? We resurrection Christians hate this moment, if the truth be told. It is filled with unknowing if we allow ourselves to linger, but we don't. We rush to the resurrection because this between-time hurts us and haunts us. It makes us uncomfortable. We don't want it. We want to fast forward to Sunday morning. We think we're being unfaithful if we don't get to the empty grave quickly.

But it's over. And the "what's next" is not on the horizon. The onlooking disciples must mourn, must grieve, must live into the disappointment. They can only hope against hope that the words they heard somewhere—where were those words?—"destroy this temple, and in three days I will raise it up" (John 2:19, NRSV) or "I am the resurrection and the life" (John 11:25, NRSV) will come in their lifetime.

What do *we* do, people of God, when we have completed what we agreed to complete, not really knowing we could, and we stand at the door of unknowing? Jesus had a sense of completion: it is finished. What about us? Are we able to believe the work really is done? Can we trust God for a future we cannot see?

In her poem-turned-book by the same name, "The Invitation," Oriah Mountain Dreamer says, "It doesn't interest me if the story you are telling me is true. I want to know if you can disappoint another to be true to yourself; if you can bear the accusation of betrayal and not betray your own soul; if you can be faithless and therefore trustworthy."[2]

Here, in this final Gospel moment, this one shining unglorified moment, Jesus betrays all the hopes of his disciples: "but we had hoped that he was the one to redeem Israel" (Luke 24:21, NRSV)—in order to be true to his call. He said, "And what should I say—'Father, save me from this hour'? No, it was for this reason that I have come to this hour" (John 12:27, NRSV). And so he accomplished the prophet's death, crucified and lynched on a tree, accomplishing what he came to do. He did not rush to resurrection. His ending—it is finished—was the beginning of a future the disciples could only dream. But until that day, they had to live with his faithlessness to them as he stood faithful to God.

I am a fan of finishers. Even when the finishing leaves us saying, "Is that it?" I'm a fan of finishers who leave us looking into an unknown future but in the sure hands of God.

A version of this sermon was preached as the final sermon in a "Last Words of Christ" series on Good Friday, 2007, at Lindenwood Christian Church (Disciples of Christ), Memphis, Tennessee. It is the last of the seven words, "It is finished."

1. Chris Dufresne, "Gators Make It 2 Straight: Florida Stakes Claim as One of Best Teams in NCAA History," *Los Angeles Times*, April 3, 2007; http://www.dailycamera.com/news/2007/apr03/gators-make-it-2-straight/ (accessed April 4, 2007).

2. Oriah Mountain Dreamer, *The Invitation* (New York: HarperCollins, 1995), 1.

27

Peace and Power:
For the Forgiveness of Sin

Denise R. Mason

JOHN 20:19-31

Jesus said to them again, "Peace be with you.
As the Father has sent me,
 so I send you." (John 20:21, NRSV)

When Jesus returns from the dead, he does three things. First, he checks in. Jesus checks in with the people he cares about and is closest to. He gives Mary an emotional and spiritual litmus test to see how she is (she fails the test, by the way). As long as she has something to do for Jesus, as long as she has some icon that represents him, it seems she can hold it together. She is not greedy. If she can't have Jesus alive, she will take him dead. Jesus checks in and finds Mary so out of it she doesn't know who she is, nor does she recognize that the One she hurts for and longs for is standing right beside her. *This is not good,* Jesus probably thinks. Then he calls her by name, "Mary!" and she is brought back to her senses. The first thing Jesus does is check in. The second thing he does is go and visit with God. Jesus tells Mary, "Do not yet hold on to me, because I have not yet ascended to the Father" (John 20:17, NRSV). In other words, I hear Jesus saying, "I am not worth holding on to until I have communed with God!" And isn't that the truth about all of us? Until we have communed with God, we really are not worth being around. The third thing Jesus does is come to be with his disciples. And through them, he comes to be with you and me too.

129

Because we know this story so well, it is easy not to hear anything unusual in it. But go with me for a moment, and I think you will notice not only the familiar but the curious too. Let's say that today we die. And we don't simply sleep away, but we suffer a tragic and horrible death. Hold on! We won't stay dead! We are resurrected. We have a new body, one that will never die. The aches and pains are gone; heartache and heartbreak—gone; worry and sleepless nights—gone. We've been resurrected from the dead, so now what do we do? I think, like Jesus, we will do the same three things: check in on our loved ones, check in with God, and then go back to hang out with our folks for a while and assure them that we are okay.

When we come back, imagine the dialogue. "Mom, I'm fine—really. I know it was horrible. I don't know how I suffered it without losing my mind. What day is it anyway? How long have I been gone? Is Dad okay? How about. . . ? Did you see the way that soldier tried to hurt me? But I didn't cry out! I was determined not to let them see me cry!" Imagine the discourse.

If the same thing that happened to Jesus happened to me or you, we would dwell on it. It would not become old news very quickly. We would take some time to process it, and we would try to figure out what it all meant. Jesus comes back, checks in with God and with loved ones, and then he completely changes the subject! He did not come back to dwell on his death. He did not come back to lament over the pain or the unfair treatment he received. He did not come back to do what so many of us might have done—either plan revenge or gloat about how things turned out. Nor did he come back to look like a martyr.

Jesus comes back to offer us two things: peace and power. Jesus says at the end of verses 19, 21, and 26, "Peace be with you." Then he says in verses 22 and 23, "Receive the Holy Spirit. If you forgive the sins of any, they are forgiven them; if you retain the sins of any, they are retained." Peace and power. Some scholars call these the keys to the office. They acknowledge that by receiving the peace of Jesus and the power to forgive sins, we are given everything we need to become disciples of Christ and uphold the apostolic office—the office of the first twelve disciples.[1] It is curious to me that instead of dwelling on the circumstances of his death and helping us to process it in a human fashion, Jesus moves us forward. By giving us peace, I think Jesus is letting us know that he is all right. By accepting his peace, we let him know that we are all right. By giving us power to forgive sins, I think Jesus is giving us the opportunity to decide exactly what his death—and therefore his life—is going to mean.

We love Jesus, and therefore the circumstances of his death could cause us to be bitter. We love Jesus. Therefore we could decide to live in fear for our own lives. We love Jesus; therefore we could become depressed. We love Jesus; therefore we could become self-righteous. Or, as Jesus suggests, we could receive the peace of Christ and the power of God.

It is interesting in Acts, Peter and the other disciples were teaching in Jerusalem, and when the high priest questioned them to remind them that they were forbidden to teach about Jesus, their response was, "God exalted him at his right hand as Leader and Savior that he might give repentance to Israel and forgiveness of sins" (Acts 5:31, NRSV). They seem to have forgotten that Jesus gave power to forgive sins directly to us. As I have studied the Gospel passage, I have come to the conclusion that forgiveness is the work of those of us who have been left behind, who profess to love God and serve Christ. It seems to me that we have a tendency to make forgiveness mostly about what God does for us. Like the disciples and apostles, we want to talk all day long about what Jesus has done for us and about what he will do for others. But, if I am listening to the Scriptures correctly, Jesus came back to talk about how we are going to be with one another.

When Thomas sees Jesus for himself, he is no longer interested in the old Jesus. Thomas had been walking around town for a week talking about putting his hand in Jesus' side and looking at the holes in Jesus' hands. But when he encounters the resurrected Jesus, when he sees him anew, he doesn't care anymore. There's a lesson there for you and me. We must let go of the circumstances of his death and the circumstances of life that are killing us every day. Instead, we must grab onto the peace and power that Christ came back to bestow. If we don't allow Jesus to get up from the grave, if we don't let Jesus put on his new body, if we don't let Jesus ascend to God, if we don't receive and welcome his new peace and his new power, then something happens to us. We remain heartbroken. We remain fearful. We remain hopeless, depressed, and vengeful. We must receive and welcome both Christ's peace and God's power to forgive. These are the keys to the office, and the power to forgive is the power to resurrect—to make right out of wrong.

How many of you have followed the Don Imus story? There is much there we could spend time on and many issues that arise from that story. But consider with me the posture of the Rutgers University athletes toward whom the attacks were made. Even though they were hurt and irate, as I am sure they were, they were the last to speak out. They never raised their voices; they never referred to him by any of the unkind images that his physical body could bring to mind. They were thoughtful—my guess is also prayerful—and by their refusal to go where their emotions were surely leading them, they offered him forgiveness. How did they do that? They did it by respectfully calling him only by his name. They did it by never asking for him to be fired from his job. They did it by not letting their families have two minutes alone with him when no one was looking! This is the same posture that Jesus leaves us with in the world.

We have been given the power to make rights out of wrongs every day that we live. We have been given the peace of the resurrected Christ. We have received the power to forgive from the same God who gave it to Christ. When we accept it, we accept the power to determine what Christ's death means. I believe that Jesus comes back as the resurrected Christ to teach us, no matter what this life puts upon us, no matter what kind of death we suffer each and every day, we—not only God—have the power to bring new life in the midst of our most desperate hour when, like Jesus, we offer one another forgiveness of sin. Oh what a world it would be if everyone who loved God in Jesus Christ honored his life, death, and resurrection by receiving what he came back to offer. Receive, people of God, the power to transform our circumstances by receiving the keys to our apostolic office: the peace of Christ and the power of God to forgive sin.

You have been reminded of the gospel of Jesus Christ. Let's make it matter. Amen!

A version of this sermon was preached at Community of Reconciliation Church, April 15, 2007, Pittsburgh, Pennsylvania.

1. *Lectionary Homiletics* 18, no. 3 (April–May 2007): 27.

28

Silent No More

Yvette Flunder

ACTS 2:1-12

All were amazed and perplexed, saying to one another, "What does this mean?" (Acts 2:12, NRSV)

Imagine a group of disjointed theological subversives still suffering scratches and bruises from journeying with Jesus down the road less traveled. This was a group for whom it was a risk to show their faces in public—they were guilty by association. They had been with Jesus, and Jesus had been arrested, tried, convicted, and executed because he had spoken truth to power and spread a welcome table.

These believers were discouraged by the recent events that had befallen their movement. Their rabbi, prophet, priest, and friend was no longer with them bodily. The crowds fell away because it had become politically and physically dangerous to be a member of the Way, and many chose a safer, more prescribed religious expression. They maintained but were afraid of the possibility of a slow but inevitable failure of the grand vision they shared with Jesus. Their company included people from diverse religious backgrounds, different classes and ethnicities, Jews and Gentiles, and women. They needed an epiphany, an outpouring of the Spirit to affirm them and clearly define what their next steps should be. Jesus sent them to the upper room.

The Spirit outpouring in that little Jerusalem apartment filled the waiting believers during what we in the Pentecostal church once called a tarry service. They tarried. They waited until they received affirmation, purpose, direction, and confidence. Almost immediately the Spirit's filling gave way to the urgency to share it. They were overwhelmed by the need to share this wonderful revelation of power and enablement, this glimpse of God. They came downstairs fearless and focused with power to share Christ with people of diverse languages and cultures. The wind of the Spirit had blown away everything that divided the speakers and the hearers. They may have felt the meaning of the words of the old spiritual: "Said I wasn't gonna tell nobody, but I couldn't keep it to myself!"

They were endowed with the Spirit much the same as Eldad and Medad in the reading from Numbers. These two brothers were not on the "A List," and it disturbed the keepers of the protocol when they became so filled with the Spirit that their witness could not be confined to the tent of meeting: unlikely recipients with an unacceptable call. Eldad and Medad extolled God's attributes and declared God's will out in the open, among the people. They prophesied without being properly ordained. They prophesied. Prophesy in the Hebrew language has powerful meanings, to foretell and forth tell. They voiced with power what God was doing and what God's plan was for Israel. When Joshua, the protocol officer, rebuked them, Moses replied, "Would that all of God's people were prophets!"

I was raised in a Joshua church where we were taught to confine the Spirit blessing to those who came into the tent, those who were part of our church and obeyed our rules. We were taught to come out from the world and be separate; to touch not, taste not, and handle not the unclean thing.

That is not the Pentecostal message; rather, the Holy Ghost, the Spirit of God will not be confined. The Holy Ghost slipped out of the tabernacle, the tent of meeting, and moved into the camp and anointed Eldad and Medad. The Spirit slipped from behind the veil that covered the Holy of Holies, slipped out of the upper room, slipped out of the Azusa Street revival, slipped out of every desperate effort to confine the Spirit to a culture, a denomination, or a doctrine and blanketed the earth with the opportunity to know the God who is not limited by the lines we draw to exclude. Some said the Spirit could not show up in Macedonia, but Paul found out God was blessing the Macedonians with the same blessing as the Jews. Some say the

Spirit is not supposed to show up in the hip-hop culture or at an AA meeting. Some would say the Spirit is not supposed to move among Asian folks, or tattooed motorcycle-riding youth, or among same-gender-loving or transgendered people, or among illegal immigrants. The Spirit is supposed to stay in the prescribed tent. Someone is saying, "Stop these people. They do not follow the rules, so they surely cannot be filled and prophesy like us!"

But the Pentecostal message is a "come out" message. Come out, come out, wherever you are. The Pentecostal message is a "go ye" message. Go ye into all the world with the message of good news. Come out of the room, down the stairs, and go ye into the street. Share the good news of God in languages and methods that are as diverse as our Creator's creation. When Peter spoke at that great Pentecostal meeting he recounted the vision of the prophet Joel, where the Spirit is poured out on all flesh. The Spirit is moving. The time is right. The stage is set. Out of our bellies, our innermost being, should flow rivers and springs of living water continuously. Glory in, Glory out; Water in, Water out; Love in, Love out; Peace in, Peace out; Spirit in, Spirit out.

We were not designed to contain the presence of God, the Spirit of God, or the grace of God. We were designed to conduct Spirit. Spirit comes to fill us and move through us, to deposit in us and then bubble up like a fountain overflowing. Spirit is moving through the earth, from home to church to community, throughout this world, throughout this cosmos, transcending time and space. Like Eldad and Medad, the upper room believers' prophesying was no longer limited to the upper room. The Spirit moved from the upper room believers on the day of Pentecost to the crowds in the street and then went home with those visiting Jerusalem for the feast. Everyone was included. It is time for Spirit-filled people to make a great mark and work to bring even more marginalized and alienated people to the table of the Lord. The work of the Spirit never has been to find ways and reasons to exclude.

We are at a defining moment now. I dare say we are on the brink of a great reformation, and a Spirit refreshing where Spirit-filled people will turn the exclusivity of religion to the inclusivity of the extravagant grace of God. We have been called to the upper room where the still-speaking God speaks through us in tongues that leaves no one out. The time is right. The stage is set.

We can't keep it to ourselves. We are taking back Pentecost. We are on the forefront of a Pentecostal evolution revolution. We are coming out of the tent, coming downstairs from the upper room, and looking for ways we can work synergistically to blend our skills and our resources and give each other support. What shall we say to these things? God is for us, so who can be against us? We've been empowered by the Spirit moving through clergy, lay folks, youth, seniors, folks of diverse ethnicities and cultures, our dancers, our poets, our Web experts, our administrators, our music folks, our folks in recovery ministry, our educators, our counselors. We have everything we need to spread the living Love of God, and we cannot keep it to ourselves! We cannot be silent anymore!

The message to everyone from the mouth of God is clear. If you are thirsty, come, believe, and drink. Drink deeply; the water will pour into you. The Spirit will fill you. The message will pour out of you, out of your belly, down the stairs, and into the camp. We cannot be silent anymore! To God be the glory!

A markedly different version of this sermon was preached on the closing day of Fellowship Conference, July 1, 2007, in Chicago.

29

A Theology of Acceptance

Jennifer Benjamin Brooks

ACTS 11:1-18

"So if God gave them the same gift as he gave us, who believed in the Lord Jesus Christ, who was I to think that I could oppose God?" (Acts 11:17, NIV)

"God grant me the serenity to accept the things I cannot change, the courage to change the things I can, and the wisdom to know the difference."[1] This much-quoted prayer, commonly called the Serenity Prayer, is not one that I say often. I have a hard time believing there's nothing or very little I should not be able to change. When it comes to living in the world, however, and perhaps dealing with some people, I too often find I need much more than the Serenity Prayer to cope with people's inability, or more often than not, their unwillingness to even try to change. Change is not easily accommodated by most people, not in the twenty-first century, and if you believe historical records, not ever. These Christians in the apostolic church, Jews by orientation, had a difficult time dealing with events requiring them to change centuries'-old thinking and practice.

This story of the Gentile Pentecost[2] appears following the raising of Tabitha. We are given Peter's retelling of the event to leaders of the Jerusalem church. Peter, following in the prophetic line exemplified by Jesus, carries out the mission of his Lord by taking the gospel to the world and baptizing in the name of the Lord Jesus. Up to this point, Peter's mission has been located only in Jerusalem, among the Jews. He is not only becoming noteworthy for his healing miracles, but the recent raising of Tabitha from the dead has put his name in lights. But now he has overstepped his bounds. He has had the nerve to allow Gentiles into the circle of Christ worshippers; he has given the uncircumcised access to the gift that, in the mind of his challengers, belonged only to the circumcised. Gentiles, not bound by Torah, were not generally circumcised. Strict adherence to Torah required that Jews remain separate from Gentiles.

But if you are doing ministry in the name of Jesus Christ and you don't get into any trouble, you need to check yourself. It seems to me that being in trouble with authorities, with leaders of the church, even with friends, is part of the legacy of true Christian service.

Peter is right on track. When he arrived in Jerusalem, "the circumcised believers criticized him," so says the text (v. 2, NIV). They are not excited about the spread of the gospel of Christ; instead, they are concerned that outsiders, "those people," have been brought into the circle that they consider theirs. Isn't it amazing the way humanity seems to be able to find reasons to separate ourselves from one another? And along with the reasons come the name calling. We create names for those we refuse to accept in order to solidify the necessity (in our minds) for separating ourselves from them. It was not enough to be Jew and Gentile; they must also be circumcised and uncircumcised. In our case, male and female and young and old are not enough to identify us. We must also be rich and poor, black and white, abled and disabled, legal or illegal, heterosexual and homosexual, Democrat and Republican, and on and on. You get the picture. We find more reasons, more dumb reasons, to divide ourselves and deny the oneness God created us to have.

Whatever gave Peter's accusers reason to think that God would not give Gentiles the same opportunity for life in Christ in all its fullness, that God would deny Gentiles or any people from benefiting from the sacrifice of Christ and of unity with God?

But the leaders of the Jerusalem church had their focus on the wrong place when they accused Peter of breaking an important taboo and eating with Gentiles.[3] Their accusation should not have been made against Peter; it should have been against God. God initiated and orchestrated the action that caused Peter's fall from grace in their eyes. All Peter did was fall in line. He had no choice. All he had to do was accept what he could not change.

138

Peter's defense to his accusers was, "It wasn't me! I didn't do it! It was God!" God had given Peter the vision that was unmistakable in its meaning, particularly when men appeared from Caesarea to take him to Cornelius's house. God prepared Peter for the change about to come. God opened Peter's eyes to the truth of God's amazing grace that was free to all people. And Peter had to accept that God's mission for his life could be fulfilled only if he allowed himself to accept change that God had already made in the makeup of God's covenantal people. "What God has made clean, you must not call profane."[4] It was a message of newness, of God's will for all people. It was a change to the status quo, a reshaping of the norm.

In a workshop on prophetic preaching given by the Styberg Preaching Institute of Garrett-Evangelical Theological Seminary in April 2007, Dr. Jeremiah Wright, pastor of Trinity United Church of Christ in Chicago, taught us to open our understanding to what it means to be prophetic in our preaching. As he reinterpreted the biblical text using the lens of prophetic witness, he adjured us to see into the Scriptures with the mind of God. Part of the instruction he gave us was a word of caution that is in line with the message in this text in Acts. He reminded us that "different does not mean deficit." That was an important part of the message that Peter received through his daytime dream.

As we look into our own situation in the church today, we are forced to admit that in too many places in our church communities we have engaged the principle of different as deficient. We also have defined groups of people as "Gentiles," different, unacceptable. They are not worthy of being among us, but worst of all, they are unworthy of receiving the grace and the power of God for their lives and their ministry in Christ's church.

As the people of God, the people for whom Christ gave his life, throughout the history of Christianity, to our shame we have made Gentiles of many groups of people. Racism is still the church's unfinished agenda; sexism and homophobia divide and try to conquer; wealthy congregations throw money at the poor but ensure poor people stay out of their sanctuaries and communities; youth are barely tolerated in the building; physically challenged people are resented for the extra expense it costs to make our buildings accessible. In all these cases, we have created a group of Gentiles. The church's twenty-first-century Gentiles are any group of persons who because of any personal characteristic are considered unfit by any person or persons within the church to a receive God's abounding, unfettered grace.

Leaders of the Jerusalem church could not accept Peter's action, but they were forced to rethink their objections when they heard who they were going up against. Who in their right mind would go up against the Holy Spirit? Do you want another indoor tornado with a little firestorm thrown in for good measure?[5] I don't think so. Peter's defense had been prepared for him, and when the Holy Spirit has your back, there's nothing that can touch you: no fear!

Peter says, "Hold on a minute; this was not my doing. Not only did God make it impossible for me to miss the message, but when I got to the place, God was there ahead of me. Before I could get my notes in good order and really preach, the Holy Spirit showed up and gave these Gentiles the exact gift that she[6] had given us on the day of Pentecost. God stopped me and reminded me of what the Teacher had said about the Holy Spirit coming on us. So I thought, *If God gave them the same gift that he gave us when we believed in the Lord Jesus Christ, who am I that I could hinder God?* I'm not crazy! I wasn't about to try to go up against God. So I fell in line and received them in the name of Lord Jesus."

Perhaps the reason we are still keeping out those we consider outside of God's grace is that we ourselves are short of acknowledging our own gift of the Holy Spirit. When was the last time you considered your life or your gift of service in Christ's kingdom to be directed, ruled, and empowered by the Holy Spirit? In many places across Christendom, the Holy Spirit is the embarrassing stepchild of the Trinity. She is too unruly, too undignified, too low-class with all that shouting and talking in tongues. We really don't want her taking over our lives and, worse yet, our church, do we? We can't control her, and she shows up uninvited and unexpected.[7]

As we look at the state of so many churches and denominations today, perhaps we need to ask ourselves a few questions about the Holy Spirit. Could it be our lack of acceptance, our outright rejection, or our unwilling tolerance of the Holy Spirit that makes us such a dead and dying church? The people to whom Peter spoke had enough sense to understand that they could not beat the Holy Spirit, so they allowed their minds to be flooded with acceptance of all people, which is the mind of God. And they began to praise God for the offer of repentance and life being extended to everyone—Jew and Gentile alike.

Perhaps our divisiveness would disappear if all of us offered our praise to God, who fills us all with grace and empowers us all by the Holy Spirit to receive God's gift of eternal life. God made us all, and God accepts us all. The God we serve in Jesus Christ does not discriminate. God knows us all, and when we accept God's offer of salvation through repentance and in baptism, God gifts each one of us with the power of the Holy Spirit. And through the power of the Holy Spirit we can begin to accept each person as a child of God, to see each person as an equal inheritor of God's bounteous love, to live as Christ decrees here on earth, to help usher in the kingdom of God, and by God's grace, to live with Christ for all eternity.

In his resurrection, Jesus Christ gave us the freedom to choose life for ourselves and, in that freedom, to accept all people as God's people, to help them to make the choice of life in Christ and accept God's precious gift for them. All are included. The choice of who will receive the gift is not ours but God's. Peter understood that message. When the Jerusalem leaders understood the situation, when at last they got it, they were silenced, struck dumb. But as soon as the message sank in, they began to praise God for God's love extended even to the Gentiles.

Peter's message is for each one of us, in the same way that God's love is for all of us. God has already given us the gift of the Holy Spirit, and God calls us to live within that spirit of love, that God-given, God-ordained, God-empowered spirit of acceptance for all people that identifies so clearly our understanding of God—our theology, if you will. My sisters and brothers, the change has already come, accept it, live into it. God has come in Jesus our Christ, and we, who have received the gift of the Holy Spirit, must offer our praise to God for Jesus' acceptance of each one of us. Now let us go forward through the love of God and by the power of the Holy Spirit to receive all people in the name of our Savior Jesus Christ. Let the Holy Spirit change anything within us that hinders us from accepting the whole people of God so that we will be able to offer our praise and thanksgiving for the unchanging, unfettered, unstinting, amazing love of God for all people and live and grow in that love. In the name of the Father and of the Son and of the Holy Spirit.

A version of this sermon, based on the story in Acts 11:1-18, was preached at the Tuesday chapel service at the Chapel of the Unnamed Faithful at Garrett-Evangelical Theological Seminary on May 1, 2007, and it is based on one of the lectionary texts for the day.

1. Wikipedia notes that "the Serenity Prayer is the common name for an originally untitled prayer written for a sermon by Reinhold Niebuhr in the 1930s or early 1940s."

2. Acts 10:44-48 records the coming of the Holy Spirit on the Gentile convert Cornelius and his household following their baptism. Just as on the day of Pentecost, these newly baptized persons began to speak in tongues, "extolling God."

3. Beyond the issue of associating with Gentiles was the problem of the eating rituals, including the washing of hands that were required of Jews.

4. The original story of Peter's dream, which is the origin of this statement, is found in Acts 10:9-16.

5. This reference relates to the coming of the Holy Spirit on the day of Pentecost.

6. The Hebrew word for God's spirit, *ruach*, is a feminine noun (also meaning breath or wind). Therefore, the preacher uses the feminine pronoun for the third person of the Trinity.

7. In *The Holy Spirit and Preaching* (Nashville: Abingdon, 1989), James Forbes gives several reasons why the Holy Spirit is an unwelcome presence in many churches.

30

Unity in Diversity

Debbie Royals

ACTS 16:16-34
They spoke the word of the Lord to him and to all who were in his house.
(Acts 16:32, NRSV)

This story in Acts that records the conversion of the prison guard and his family, when read together with our Gospel text, invites us to understand what our Elder Brother, Jesus Christ, meant when he taught us about loving one another. His life and teachings intended that we unite as a community, loving one another while celebrating the diversity of God's creation.

As an indigenous woman, a Native American—Pascua Yaqui, I am moved by these readings, particularly because I hear them through the contemporary stories of the lives of indigenous people living in America and the world. One of the wonders of Scripture is its relevance for our lives. These stories continue to challenge us to be the people our Creator intended for us to be—to be transformed through love celebrating all diversity.

The story in Acts places Paul and Silas, citizens of Rome, in the Roman colony of Philippi in Macedonia. They have come there because they were invited by Lydia, a woman from Thyatira.

Paul and Silas are not anonymous for very long. A young girl, gifted with psychic abilities, proclaims that Paul and Silas are messengers of God. Paul and Silas discover that the young girl is a slave and

143

that her masters are using her gift for personal gain. Paul releases her from enslavement by ordering the spirit that possesses her out. What comes next is the irony of the story. Paul and Silas are taken into custody, beaten, and then locked up for righting an injustice.

Paul and Silas do not despair, nor are they silenced. In fact, their singing and praying rock the world. An earthquake shakes the prison so violently that the doors fly open. The sleeping guard wakes up and panics, assuming the prisoners have escaped. That guard knows that his punishment will likely cost him his life, so he decides just to take his own life and avoid prolonging the inevitable. But Paul calls out to him that no prisoners have left their cells. The prison guard, transformed by the experience, is baptized, along with his whole family.

It is not a stretch for me to understand how Paul and Silas might have been seen as foreigners in their own land. Indigenous people have experienced foreignness for centuries as people from other lands displaced us either forcefully or by simply acting as if we were not here. Native Americans can tell you that our gifts are often exploited for someone else's gain. Take, for example, all the knock-off jewelry made to look like the silver and turquoise jewelry crafted by Native Americans. Or the numbers of New Age practices that have adopted sacred ceremonial traditions, such as burning sage, sweat lodge ceremonies, or vision quests.

Just as it was ironic that Paul and Silas were imprisoned over a justice issue, so is it ironic that more Native Americans now live in urban areas and not on reservations. And there is irony in the demand for or use of traditional Native American ceremonial elements when these are the same things that have been categorized as pagan or superstitious.

I am often asked by both Native and non-Native peoples how it is possible to be both Native and Christian. This question is still at the heart of the struggles that manifest themselves in racism, violence, war, and self-destructive behaviors. The current issues challenging many people of faith come from our inability to allow people who are different than we are, people who think differently than we do, or people whose gifts are misunderstood, to transform us into the more loving and accepting people that God intended us to be. Is unity possible in the church and the world in the midst of our differences and controversies? Certainly this is the hope of resurrection and Christ incarnate.

144

What does it mean to be united? In Madeleine L'Engle's book *A Wrinkle in Time*, she describes a planet where everything is alike. On this planet a character representation of evil, IT, sets the purpose and direction for all people. IT understands this conformity in contrast to the vibrancy of God's creative world.[1] IT knows the face of evil as its own.

IT's sameness is not the unity of the gospel. The unity of the gospel is much harder. It requires us to live into the diversity of God's creation. It requires us to be reconciled with love and compassion to a higher purpose—one that results in unity. Contrary to popular thought, unity that enlarges the kingdom of God is not meant to impose the melting-pot mentality that destroys cultural, theological, and social distinctions. Unity that celebrates the diversity of God's creation comes from living into the two great commandments—to love God and to love one another as God loves us.

The Gospel reading invites us into unity that comes from being with God just as God is with us. This awareness of God in our lives and in all of creation, though understood in many ways by different cultures and religions, has one unifying product—shalom—not merely peace, but as our presiding bishop Katharine Jefferts Schori describes, "Shalom [that] has to do with the restoration of all creation to right relationship with God."[2] God's unity comes from relating to one another inclusively, affirming each person's expression of God in them and God with them. It is God's call and prayer for us all to unite in mission, to release those imprisoned by poverty, lack of education, and gender inequality. It is to work on behalf of those who lack adequate health care, causing child mortality, poor maternal health, and diseases like HIV/AIDS, malaria, tuberculosis, and others that ravage God's people. It is to respond to environmental injustices. And it is to do it together until global partnerships are developed.[3]

The prayer that Jesus prays in the Gospel is one of unity and witness to the love of God in the world:

> "Righteous Father, the world does not know you, but I know you; and these know that you have sent me. I made your name known to them, and I will make it known, so that the love with which you have loved me may be in them, and I in them." (John 17:25-26, NRSV)

When you read the Gospel of John in Greek, you realize how similar the words "one" and "in" are to each other, but more important is how repetitively they appear, making it almost impossible to miss the point. And, as in our reading from Revelation, it is God's glory that comes through when we are united in God's love.

This love is what makes us a serving community united in one accord and mission. This love is what showed through in Paul and Silas to the community in Philippi. This love is what shines through each of us as God's children. Can you imagine how bright the beacon of that love is when we are all shining together—beaming with love through our actions—one in mission?

This is the prayer Jesus prayed in our Gospel today. This is God glorified in Revelation. This is the unity that celebrates the diversity of all creation. To God be the praise! Amen.

A condensed version of this sermon appeared on Sermons That Work, an online resource for small congregations. Used by permission of the author.

1. Madeleine L'Engle, *A Wrinkle in Time* (New York: Bantam Doubleday Dell, 1962), 145–62.

2. Katharine Jefferts Schori, *Presiding Bishop's Credo*, December 30, 2006.

3. United Nations Millennium Development Goals, adopted by the Episcopal Church at General Convention, 2006.

31

It's in the Seed

Veronica Martin Thomas

2 CORINTHIANS 9:6-7

But this I say: He who sows sparingly will also reap sparingly, and he who sows bountifully will also reap bountifully. So let each one give as he purposes in his heart, not grudgingly or of necessity; for God loves a cheerful giver. (2 Corinthians 9:6-7, NKJV)

A friend told me that when she was a child, her mother and father never owned their own home. They lived in public, government-owned and government-managed housing. Yard area was at a premium. She said that no matter where they lived, her father always kept a garden. Her father said soil is always different, and he had to use various techniques to get it ready for planting. He had to remove grass, rock, stone, and other plants that covered the garden site. Her father had to break up the soil, digging down between eight and twelve inches, a feat sometimes easier said than done. Next steps included turning the soil over, mixing in fertilizer to improve the soil, and raking the soil thoroughly, allowing it to become fine and smooth. It took all these steps just to prepare to plant a garden.

What does God have to do to our heart's soil to get us ready to plant good seed? The upper layer of the soil gives food to plants that have short roots, like small grains and grasses. Topsoil also contains bacteria necessary for plants to grow. Plants need all three soil levels to continue to grow. It didn't matter what kind of soil my friend's father began with, he could prepare the soil for growth. Likewise, we need the triune, three-in-one God for our spiritual growth. God will keep us fertile for growth. After all the preparation of the soil, my friend's father discovered plant growth depends on the seed. It's in the seed. The seed has to be planted to receive a harvest.

In our text today, Paul is dealing with the offering for the saints at Jerusalem. He encourages the Corinthians to be generous by using the Macedonians as examples. At the same time, Paul encourages the Macedonians by quoting the Corinthians. But he is just a little afraid the Corinthians may let him down! Paul had been promoting a fund-raising effort on behalf of the needy in Jerusalem, and the Corinthians made some commitments to the project but seemed to have lost their momentum.

So Paul encouraged the Christians in Corinth to seize the moment, respond in compassion, and demonstrate in a tangible way their unity with Jewish Christians in Jerusalem. This encouragement is typical of Paul and of his great heart. Paul never criticized one church to another. He praised each to the other. There is no better standard by which to test a person than whether he or she delights in retelling the best or the worst about others.

Paul's great desire is that the Corinthian gift be ready and not have to be collected at the last minute. How dreadful if the poverty-stricken Macedonians should arrive at Corinth and find that the church whose examples had been quoted to them had given a miserly contribution! In such circumstances the Corinthians would stand in shame, and so would Paul. So Paul sends his colleagues in advance to ensure the gift would be ready, not as a gift extorted from them against their will, but as a willing gift, literally a blessing. These blessings issue from human love in response to divine grace, which will lead to joy as well as help for the recipients.

An old Latin proverb says, "He gives twice who gives quickly."[1] It is true still. The finest gifts are those made before they are requested. It was while we were yet sinners that Christ died for us. God hears our prayers even before we speak them. And we should act toward our fellow humans as God acts toward us.

Paul shows us three things about planting good seeds. First, giving is like sowing seed. A seed sown produces a harvest. He who sows sparingly will also reap sparingly. Whoever heard of a farmer so mean as to scatter only a few seeds in his field? What a miserable harvest it would be!

So it is in the realm of giving. To give little is to reap little—both in one's own life and in the lives of others. The same thought is expressed even more strongly in Galatians 6:7, the context of which is closely related to this passage. There is a more profound relation between a person's giving and his or her spiritual welfare than is sometimes realized. Paul wants us to face the issue in relation to God and his kingdom. Giving is an investment in our eternal future. We must remember: the bigger the planting, the greater the harvest.

Second, giving is personal. The giver's attitude is important. To give reluctantly or under compulsion is out of keeping with the Christian's experience of God and with the teaching of the Bible. God wants us to be obedient, as the children of Israel obeyed God's instruction through Moses to bring an offering to build God's tabernacle, according to Exodus. God isn't interested in money given grudgingly. This offering must be given with a willing heart. We should ask not only, "What must we do, but what may we do for God?" A basic principle of giving is established in Exodus. Offerings to the Lord should be voluntary and spontaneous. The Hebrew text reads literally, "whose heart urges him [or her] to give." Wanting to is still basic in dedicating anything to the Lord. We sometimes dream of what we would give to God if we were wealthy. Moses' instructions to Israel are a healthy reminder. We can give only from what we have. When we give willingly, we please God and find joy in giving. Everyone is extended the invitation to give. The response was so great that Moses had to stop the outpouring of gifts. Today, too, if we would give of what we have, there would be more than enough to do all God commands. It's in the seed.

Third, giving is an expression of trust. God is able to meet our needs and to provide much more so we can give joyfully and without fear. Giving stimulates prayer. The recipient praises God and prays for the giver. God loves a cheerful giver, and the Christian knows that, because that is the spirit in which God has ever treated his children.

Paul turns our attention to a familiar scene. The harvest image stresses the results of choices made during the planting process. It is the farmer who decides how much to plant. A few seeds will produce a small crop. The analogy, of course, is clear. If we give grudgingly and give little, we can expect little. But if we are generous, the results from our giving will be greater. It is we who decide the size of the response and the effectiveness of our giving. A generous heart marks evidence of the Holy Spirit's work in our lives. The giving of our time, energy, and financial resources is the expression of a grateful heart. God's blessing is much more than a prosperity message for physical gain. The message is to empower us to sow in fertile ground, which in turn will reap a holistic harvest.

What are we planting? God is looking for individuals willing to plant seeds of love, shown in our actions. God is looking for good seed to multiply: If we sow joy, we will reap strength. "The joy of the LORD is your strength" (Nehemiah 8:10, NKJV). It's in the seed! If we sow peace, we will reap security. "The peace of God, which surpasses all understanding, will guard your hearts and minds through Christ Jesus" (Philippians 4:7, NKJV). It's in the seed! If we sow longsuffering, we will reap patience. "Count it all joy when you fall into various trials, knowing that the testing of your faith produces patience" (James 1:2-3, NKJV). It's in the seed! If we sow gentleness, we will reap good conduct. "Let your gentleness be known to all men. The Lord is at hand" (Philippians 4:5, NKJV). It's in the seed! If we sow goodness, we will reap character. "O my soul, you have said to the Lord, 'You are my Lord, My goodness is nothing apart from You'" (Psalm 16:2, NKJV). It's in the seed! If we sow faithfulness, we will reap confidence. "He did not waver at the promise of God through unbelief, but was strengthened in faith, giving glory to God, and being fully convinced that what He had promised He was also able to perform" (Romans 4:20-21, NKJV). It's in the seed! If we sow meekness, we will reap humility. "Blessed are the meek, for they shall inherit the earth" (Matthew 5:5, NKJV). It's in the seed! If we sow self-control, we will reap victory. "In this you rejoice, even if now for a little while you have had to suffer various trials, so that the genuineness of your faith— being more precious than gold that, though perishable, is tested by fire—may be found to result in praise and glory and honor when Jesus Christ is revealed . . . for you are receiving the outcome of your faith, the salvation of your souls" (1 Peter 1:6-7, 9, NRSV).

A seed was planted in the womb of Mary that produced our Savior. A seed was planted for his resurrection and our deliverance. The songwriter reminds us, "You can't beat God's giving, no matter how you try, and just as sure as you are living and the Lord is in heaven on high. The more you give, the more he gives to you. But keep on giving because it's really true that you can't beat God giving no matter how you try. Should we receive and never give? The Savior died that we might live. His life on Calvary he gladly gave; our sinful souls to save."[2] It's in the seed!

A version of this sermon was preached at New Bethel Church of God in Christ (2004), Coleman Place Presbyterian Church (March 2006), Mt. Gilead Missionary Baptist Church (December 2006), and Messiah Presbyterian Church (January 2007), all in Norfolk, Virginia.

1. *Publius Syrus Minmus* by Langius in "Polyanth-Noviss," 382. Old Latin proverb.
2. Doris Akers, "You Can't Beat God's Giving," *The New National Baptist Hymnal* (Nashville: Baptist Publishing Board, 1977), 383.

32
Forging Prophetic Alliances

Loida I. Martell-Otero

EPHESIANS 4:1-7, 11-13

There is one body and one Spirit, just as you were called to the one hope of your calling. (Ephesians 4:4, NRSV)

In a postmodern age, given the political and social realities that face this nation in particular and the world in general, the word *alliance* has taken an almost pejorative tone. People form alliances for all kinds of reasons. In some societies, they often are associated with military might—groups of people forging relationships with each other to fight a common enemy. In many others, they are formed by groups, families, tribes, or states with common goals or legacies. Thus, alliances too often are formed to enforce hegemony or reinforce homogeneity: like likes like. These are what I call worldly alliances. Given these political and social realities, can we as Christians envision a different kind of alliance? Can we envision one that is prophetic, that celebrates not homogeneity but diversity, one that leads not to death and violence but to the formation of community and the sustenance of life?

I believe that is why we have gathered here: to articulate new ways in which African American, Asian and Asian American, Latina, and women of color in general can forge prophetic and healthy alliances with white women in theological education. It is not an easy task. There is a long history among us. There are wounds of the past and present, worldviews, cultures, languages, and myriad other things that make such alliances difficult to forge. The temptation is to forge

152

worldly alliances, ones that can help individual homogenous or hege-monic groups defy each other. Yet our call is not for worldly alliances but rather prophetic ones. And so here we are, responding as the prophet Isaiah, "Here am I" (Isaiah 6:8, NRSV). This response, how-ever, leads to the question: How do we forge such alliances? Can we envision a new way of being with each other? Put in more biblical and theological terms, can we become a body of Christ in the midst of our diversity? I believe that Ephesians 4:1-7 and 11-13, in addressing the theme of unity, can also speak to us about forging alliances in the midst of diversity.

To begin with, the author of Ephesians makes the profound obser-vation that unity is not a choice we make. To forge an alliance is not something we do, like when we choose to go to the supermarket or to the dentist. To forge an alliance, to become one, is not a choice but a vocation. Vocation is derived from the root words *vocatio* (to be sum-moned) and *vocare* (to be called).[1] And because it is *vocatio/vocare,* a calling, it involves two important elements. The first thing we must be aware of is that forging alliances is a calling made by God. But the God who calls is not just any God. The God who calls us is a Trinitarian God. God who is community in Godself, God who is Diversity-in-One—Parent, Son, and Holy Spirit—has created us a diverse commu-nity that we may be one. But if indeed it is God who calls us to community with God and with each other because God is community in Godself, then we must ask ourselves: How can we claim to know God, indeed claim to be children of God, if we do not live as one? Can we truly consider ourselves faithful servants of the Most High who has called us if we live in separation from our sisters and brothers simply because they are not like us, or do not talk like us, or do not look like us, or whatever other qualifications we put on people?

Some of you have expressed the deeply felt pain and frustration that arise when one encounters the walls of divisiveness, injustice, inhu-manity, rejection, and intolerance. You have asked, "How do we go beyond the rhetoric?" How, indeed, do we do more than talk the talk rather than walk the walk? The text in Ephesians reminds us that we can go beyond rhetoric only if we acknowledge, if we insist that jus-tice is not a choice but a vocation. Indeed, it is a demand by God who is community in Godself that we be conduits of God's love and com-munity. And in so doing, we become the firstfruits, a prophetic (and

153

even, dare I say, a teaching) model for the world and in the world. We must accept the fact that we also become the thorn in the side of those who would complacently accept the status quo because it benefits them, or because it is how things are, or because they fear more those in the world than the One who created the world (see 1 John 4:4). It frightens those in the world when they are faced with concrete evidence of an alternative way of being and living, because it challenges those who uphold the status quo to make a commitment and forces them to choose to "not be conformed to this [present age] but be transformed" (Romans 12:2, NRSV) by the power of God's Spirit. Let us therefore heed the call of God, who summons us to be allied prophets.

Second, the author of Ephesians reminds us that forging an alliance is not only a vocation. Precisely because it is *vocatio/vocare*, it is also a gift from the Lord who has gifted us with God's own fullness of being. Alliances cannot be achieved without grace and the outpouring of the Spirit in our midst. As grace and vocation, it is not a momentary job or a temporal relationship. Prophetic alliance is a lifelong commitment; a life script entrusted to us by our triune God.[2] To forge a prophetic alliance is to acknowledge God's vocation to be one body. That call to one body is a challenge. Yet to become one body should not be seen, or experienced, as a burden but rather a joy; a gift of love given to us, poured out upon us, by the One who *is* love. It is an unfolding of God's vision in us and through us.[3] This vision of God is the true nature of Pentecost. And because it is a gift, the outpouring of the Spirit graces us with charisms: gifts given to the body to aid in its becoming one made of many and not simply one more among the many.

We are horrified when we hear on the news of some dismembered body that has been found. We are horrified by the violence implied. We grieve for a life lost unnecessarily and tragically. But we Christians sometimes lose sight of the horror that we must present to the world when we, as the body of Christ, live as a dismembered, disjointed, and divided community. Our body suffers from fractures of the *-isms* that assail us, even as we purport to desire to heal the world! The body's brokenness is visible in the many mangled and suffering communities that populate our world. Its fissures are clearly present when women of color give witness that the few times they feel valued, affirmed, and loved are in gatherings such as these. Imagine! Women theologians who are supposed to be enfleshed witnesses of God's presence are not even deemed human by those who supposedly reflect on God! This passage reminds and challenges us that we are called to be a whole body of Christ. But because God knows our brokenness, God also provides for our healing: God enables us to forge an alliance, through the gifts of the Spirit. It is grace.

There are two particular words in this pericope that underscore this grace for me. In verse 12, we find the word "equip," or *perfeccionar,* "to perfect" in the Spanish version. The other is the word "maturity" (*perfecto* in the Spanish version) in verse 13. "Perfect" in the biblical sense means "to make whole" or "complete." "Equip" here is the translation for the Greek word *katartismos,* which can also be translated as "setting the broken bones."[4] In medicine, there are different classifications of broken bones. A simple fracture is when a bone breaks into two clean pieces and can be easily mended by a cast or splint. A comminuted fracture is more complex; the bone is broken in two places or more and therefore needs a more aggressive intervention. The most dangerous fracture is the compound fracture. Here the bone breaks through the skin, compounding the problem by damaging different layers of tissue and exposing the body to infection.

Our communities, indeed the body of Christ, suffer from compound fractures and fissures that are generational, social, political, cultural, linguistic, and so on. They are not simple fractures but deep and complex ones. To treat them as simple fractures potentially can do more harm than good, precisely because there are no easy answers, no one way to deal with them. To heal such profound brokenness may seem, at first blush, to be beyond our capacities. The situations we face may seem hopeless. This is why this text in Ephesians is so prophetic for me, for in the text lie words of hope. On the one hand, the passage underscores that such healing does not depend on us alone (and certainly not individually). It is God's Spirit who moves and pours grace and wholeness. On the other hand, it reminds us that transformation cannot happen without us. We are summoned, called, to be part of this outpouring of grace.

I believe that this understanding is nuanced well in Spanish: the Spirit of God grants us gifts *a fin de* (with a goal to) *perfeccionar.* That is to say, the complex of charisms is given to make whole, to heal that which is disjointed in the body. Thus, all of us need to partake of them, and we cannot be whole unless *all* of us are present. The body cannot be if its parts are at war with each other. A body that is broken up cannot thrive, cannot grow, and cannot live a full life. We cannot exist in pieces or apart from each other. So this is our calling: to realize that we cannot live in Christ, that we cannot claim to be servants of the triune God and continue to accept the compounded fractures of our sisters, our brothers, and our communities as if they were business as usual. We are called to transform business as usual. We are called to cry out to the Lord and ask of God, "Come, Holy Spirit, and pour out your anointing and heal our fractures, and make us whole. Heal our brokenness so that we can grow to the measure of the full stature of Christ." And this healing can be done only through the grace of the God who has called us to be one made of many, and not many parts mangled in one.

This calling by God is why forging a prophetic alliance is ultimately a salvific process. It is why it cannot simply be a choice. We are called by the One who is community in self to be community with God. We are called to be healed that we may be community with each other. We are granted life so that we can live as one joined in love. This is our calling. This is our gift. This is our hope. Amen.

A version of this sermon was preached at the Association of Theological Schools-sponsored Women in Leadership Seminar *on "Racial/Ethnic Women and White Women Building Alliances in Theological Education," October 21–23, 2005, in Pittsburgh, Pennsylvania.*

1. George Arthur Buttrick, *The Interpreter's Dictionary of the Bible*, (Nashville, TN: Abingdon Press, 1962) s.v., "vocation."

2. Herbert Alphonso, *Discovering Your Personal Vocation: The Search for Meaning through the Spiritual Exercises* (New York: Paulist Press, 2001).

3. I am grateful to Dr. Renata Furst for her insight into vocation as an "unfolding of a particular, unrepeatable, unique grace." Personal communication with author, April 2005.

4. Markus Barth, *Ephesians 4–6 Anchor Bible Commentary*, vol. 34A, (Garden City, NY: Doubleday, 1974), 439.

33

"In Spite of" Discipleship

Minh-Hanh Nguyen

1 THESSALONIANS 1:2-7
We always give thanks to God for all of you and mention you in our prayers, constantly remembering before our God and Father your work of faith and labor of love and steadfastness of hope in our Lord Jesus Christ. For we know, brothers and sisters, beloved by God, that he has chosen you, because our message of the gospel came to you not in word only, but also in power and in the Holy Spirit and with full conviction; just as you know what kind of persons we proved to be among you for your sake. And you became imitators of us and of the Lord, for in spite of persecution you received the word with joy inspired by the Holy Spirit, so that you became an example to all the believers in Macedonia and in Achaia. (1 Thessalonians 1:2-7, NRSV)

The reaffirming words from Paul to the Thessalonians is so befitting our mood this Sunday morning, after a wonderful weekend of engaging in ample opportunities for learning, listening to each other's stories, taking part in exhilarating musical expression, praying alone, praying for one another, meeting new friends, and reconnecting with those we hadn't seen in a while. What a mountaintop experience!

I can imagine the elation felt by the recipients of such an upbuilding message praising their discipleship efforts from top leaders Paul, Silvanus, and Timothy. Wouldn't we be elated for days if we received an e-mail like today's text from our bishop's office?

By sharing our stories, our experience in Christian apprenticeship, we have in essence been saying to one another the same reaffirming words Paul and company said to the Thessalonians; maybe Paul's words then and our story now would not have meant much if they did not include the "in spite of" moments expressed in verse 6: "And you became imitators of us and of the Lord, for in spite of persecution you received the word with joy inspired by the Holy Spirit."

Here in the United States, we have freedom of religion. We are not persecuted by the government authorities as are some in other countries, or as in Jesus' time, but we do experience other forms of persecution. That persecution may be a form of North American, European Lutheran cultural persecution from our peers. Our persecution may come in being branded as un-Lutheran. The Vietnamese clergy in the evangelical Christian community in Orange County for a long time were not comfortable with me in their midst because I had also invited many Buddhist monks, among leaders of other Vietnamese spiritual traditions, to my ordination. I am told I sound like a Buddhist, while I actually use the vernacular spiritual language that would touch the hearts of non-Christian Vietnamese. The legal charges brought against All Saints Episcopal Church in Pasadena at this time may be considered a form of persecution for doing what they're called to do as Christ's disciples, preaching peace and social justice in both words and deeds.[1]

The old hymn "Just as I Am" that we sang last night was one that also speaks to that "in spite of" nature of our God. Yes, these are the grace-filled "in spite of" moments in our journey of discipleship that strengthen our faith, our hope, and our trust in God's unconditional love and the power of the Holy Spirit. In spite of all the obstacles we have to overcome in the ways we proclaim the good news of Jesus Christ, the power of the Holy Spirit is always there for us to draw from, so that we can be God's hands, God's voice, God's feet, God's instruments for our ministries to the world as apprentices of Christ's way of life.

I'm so thankful for God's instruments and gifts in every member of this event's organizing team who use multimedia to help us make connections with all our senses. Items that help us make these connections include the fishing nets as centerpieces and this substantial earthy cross necklace. Whenever we touch it or look at it, it's a reminder for us of our commitment to proclaim the good news of Jesus Christ as part of a disciple's life—no matter what the "in spite of" twist and turn of our journey may be.

158

Bishop Murray Finck (ELCA–Pacifica Synod) told us about the ministry situation for the Lutheran Church in Hong Kong. After the territory of Hong Kong was returned to the government of mainland China, every inch of land in Hong Kong came under government control. The Lutheran church of Hong Kong applied for a permit to build a church building in a community. They were told first to survey the community's needs at that time and organize to meet that need first; then the request for building a church would be considered. The survey indicated the community needed a laundry facility. The Hong Kong church agreed to set up such a facility if it was given space for it. There was a nine-story building nearby that was being used partly by the government.

And so the government gave the church a nearby nine-story building to build a laundry facility. One type of community service led to another. To meet the needs of the local residents, the Lutheran Church of Hong Kong, in a few years, was given all nine floors of the building to provide various services to the people in the neighborhood. After taking notice of how the church served the needs of the local community, the Hong Kong government offered land and the permit for the church to build its church building.

The real reason for the Hong Kong authorities' prerequisite for the church building permit may never be known to us, yet it caused the Lutheran Church in Hong Kong to backtrack and reclaim its original Christian discipleship; it caused the Hong Kong Lutheran Church to redefine the Good News it was supposed to be proclaiming. Their endeavors, although initially not by choice, were radical—radical in the sense that it went back to the roots of proclaiming the Good News. In essence, these practical demands by the authorities were saying, practice what you think is good news to the people's lives; let them decide if what you do is truly good news to them first. Then we can talk about letting you preach that religion to the community.

True discipleship happens when we are transformed from benefiting from the Good News to being good news ourselves to others, as we work for justice and peace in all the earth and obey the teaching of our Lord Jesus Christ's command as motivation for all that we do—"You shall love the Lord your God with all your heart, and with all your soul, and with all your mind, and . . . love your neighbor as yourself" (Matthew 22:37, 39). This morning, as we return to our

respective ministries and lives, may the power of the Holy Spirit continue to fan aglow the flames of discipleship in each one of us,
through our "in spite of" times, and indeed through all the days of
our lives. Amen.

*A version of this sermon was preached at the "Living into the Cross"
conference of the Evangelical Lutheran Church in America, Chicago,
on November 19, 2006.*

1. All Saints Episcopal Church came under scrutiny and risked losing its tax-
exempt status based on an anti-war sermon that was preached just days before
the 2004 presidential election. See http://abclocal.go.com/kabc/story?section=
news/local&id=5671114 (accessed March 23, 2008).

About the Contributors

Donna E. Allen founded and pastors New Revelation Community Church in Oakland, California. She holds a PhD from the Graduate School of Religion, Vanderbilt University, where she wrote a dissertation titled "Toward a Womanist Homiletic: Katie Cannon, Alice Walker, and Emancipatory Proclamation." An assistant professor of preaching and worship, she teaches at Lancaster Theological Seminary, Lancaster, Pennsylvania.

Liala Ritsema Beukema currently serves Lake View Lutheran Church, Chicago. A graduate of Western Theological Seminary, Holland, Michigan, she is an ordained pastor of the Reformed Church in America. She previously served as pastor of The Church of the Good News, an RCA congregation located in one of Chicago's public housing communities. She has a spouse and two children who keep her humble.

Dionne P. Boissière, a graduate of Union Theological Seminary in New York City, currently serves as associate director of development and alumni/ae relations at the seminary. She also is an associate minister at New Hope Baptist Church in Danbury, Connecticut. Of Trinidad/Tobago descent, she teaches in both Abyssinian Baptist Church Institute for Christian Education and Trinity Baptist Church Bible Institute (Bronx, New York).

Valerie Bridgeman Davis is associate professor of Hebrew Bible Homiletics & Worship at Memphis Theological Seminary. She founded and directs the seminary's theology and arts institute. In addition, she serves as general editor for the United Methodist Church's Africana Worship project; is on the editorial board of the *Biblia Africana Hebrew Bible Commentary*; and is the

161

generative mother of "The Tribe," a collective of artists working on justice as a spiritual discipline. She is a performing artist and widely published poet. Ordained by the Church of God (Anderson, Indiana), she holds degrees from Trinity University (BA, double major in religion and communication); Austin Presbyterian Theological Seminary (MDiv); and Baylor University (PhD, biblical studies).

Gennifer Benjamin Brooks is Ernest and Bernice Styberg Professor of Preaching at Garrett-Evangelical Theological Seminary. A native of Trinidad, West Indies, and an ordained elder in the New York Conference of the United Methodist Church, she holds degrees from Pace University (BB and MBA), New Brunswick Theological Seminary (MDiv [summa cum laude] and DMin), and Drew University (PhD, liturgical studies).

MarQuita A. Carmichael Burton is the married mother of one son. She has served as an associate minister at Pilgrim Journey Baptist Church and pastor of the Vineyard Ministries in Richmond, Virginia. MarQuita is an Arlington, Virginia, native who earned her MDiv from the Samuel DeWitt Proctor School of Theology at Virginia Union University and is a resident chaplain of clinical pastoral education at the UCLA Medical Center.

E. Anne Henning Byfield (MDiv), itinerant elder, is the first female presiding elder of the South District Indiana Conference, African Methodist Episcopal Church. A third-generation preacher, she pastored three churches. She is a poet, published author, songwriter, and president of annehenningbyfield, inc, a consulting company that provides public speaking, leadership, and organizational transformation as well as executive development and coaching.

Helen Bessent Byrd holds degrees from Union Theological Seminary & Presbyterian School of Christian Education [Richmond] (MDiv), University of Connecticut (PhD), Temple University (ME), and Berea College (BA). She retired from Norfolk State University, where she served as professor, department chair, and director of numerous external grants in the school of education. Helen is an ordained elder at Messiah Presbyterian Church in Norfolk, Virginia, and has served on numerous presbytery, synod, and general assembly boards and committees in the Presbyterian Church (USA).

Elizabeth Conde-Frazier is an ordained American Baptist minister with more than ten years experience in the local church. She currently is associate professor of religious education at the Claremont School of Theology. She also teaches at the Latin American Bible Institute in La Puente, California. She is author of *Hispanic Bible Institutes* and coauthor of *A Many Colored Kingdom: Multicultural Dynamics for Spiritual Formation.*

Holly Haile Davis, of the Shinnecock Nation, is the first Native American female ordained minister of Word and sacrament in the Presbyterian Church (PC/USA). She is granddaughter of the late Chief and Mrs. Thunder Bird. She holds a degree from the University of Dubuque Theological Seminary (MDiv). Among other assignments, she served as pastor at the Ute Mountain Presbyterian Church, Towaoc, Colorado, and is founding pastor of the Padoquohan Medicine Lodge, Inc., an interfaith fellowship on the Shinnecock Indian Reservation. She taught Presbyterian polity at Cook College and Theological School in Tempe, Arizona.

Lisa Wilson Davison holds degrees from Brite Divinity School at Texas Christian University (MDiv) and Vanderbilt University (PhD). She is professor of the First Testament at Lexington Theological Seminary. An Anglo woman from a small town in southwestern Virginia, Lisa has two passions: studying women in the First Testament and speaking on behalf of people who have been excluded from church and society by people who misuse the Bible. She is author of *Preaching the Women of the Bible* (Chalice Press).

Yvette Flunder, a San Francisco native, is founding and presiding bishop of Refuge Ministries/The Fellowship, a multidenominational fellowship of 110 primarily African American Christian leaders and laity representing 56 churches and faith-based organizations throughout the United States and Africa. She was consecrated in 2003. Her roots are in the Church of God in Christ, and she holds ordination in the United Church of Christ and is the founding pastor of City of Refuge Community Church UCC. The congregation has a significant ministry to people living with HIV/AIDS. She holds degrees from Pacific School of Religion, Berkeley (MA) and San Francisco Theological Seminary (DMin). She recorded and performed with the Walter Hawkins and the Family and the Love Center Choir. She serves on several boards and is a much sought-after published preacher, educator, conference speaker, and singer.

Wil Gafney, PhD, is associate professor of Hebrew and Old Testament at The Lutheran Theological Seminary at Philadelphia. She graduated from Earlham

College, Howard University School of Divinity, and Duke University (graduate certificate in women's studies and PhD in Hebrew Bible). She is an Episcopal priest, a member of the African Episcopal Church of St. Thomas, and the Dorshei Derekh Reconstructionist Minyan of the Germantown Jewish Center, both in Philadelphia. Her examination of female prophets, *Daughters of Miriam,* is available from Fortress Press.

Emily C. Hassler is senior pastor of Washington Park United Church of Christ, Denver, Colorado. A graduate of Austin Presbyterian Theological Seminary, she is fond of reconstructing scriptural stories in the light of her feminist deconstruction tendencies. She has served as an adjunct professor at Iliff School of Theology. Long a lover of Jesus, she feels far more ambiguous about most organized religion.

Phyllis Thompson Hilliard was licensed to preach in 1991 and ordained as a staff pastor in 2006 by her husband, Bishop Donald Hilliard Jr., senior pastor of Cathedral International in Perth Amboy, New Jersey. Pastor Phyllis Thompson Hilliard has directed the Cathedral women's ministry for the past fifteen years. Known for her demonstrative preaching and teaching, she also founded and directs Winsome Ministries, Inc., begun in 2002. Also an author, she regards as her greatest accomplishment mothering her three adult daughters, Leah, Charisma, and Destiny.

Carla Jean-McNeil Jackson, Esq., is a licensed minister and practicing attorney. She received degrees from Occidental College (BA), University of Richmond (JD), and Samuel DeWitt Proctor School of Theology, Virginia Union University (MDiv, magna cum laude). Carla also is an accomplished soloist and ensemble singer whose talents have been praised in the United States and abroad, including a four-month tour of Italy in the musical *Sister Act 2.* She is an associate minister at St. Paul's Baptist Church, Richmond, Virginia, where she serves as the coordinator for the ministers' training program.

Anne-Marie Jeffery grew up in the Anglican Church in Antigua, West Indies. She worked as a physicist until 2001, when she accepted a call to ordained ministry. From 2004 to 2007, she served as urban missioner, the Episcopal Church of the Epiphany in downtown Washington, D.C. Currently, she is priest in charge at St. James Episcopal Church, Bowie, Maryland, and Episcopal chaplain at Bowie State University.

EunJoung Joo was born in South Korea, where she was raised as Korean Methodist. She came to the United States in 2001 and joined the United Methodist Church. She holds degrees from Wesley Theological Seminary (MTS) and Methodist Theological Seminary (MDiv). She currently serves as associate pastor at Glen Burnie United Methodist Church in Glen Burnie, Maryland.

Portia Wills Lee founded and serves as senior pastor of Trinity Tabernacle Baptist Church, formerly Trinity African Baptist, in Mableton, Georgia. She has received many awards for ministry activism and is a member of several civic organizations. She mentors and advises seminary students at Candler School of Theology, Emory University. She holds degrees from Middle Tennessee State University (BA) and Candler (MDiv, pastoral care/counseling concentration). A native of Clarksville, Tennessee, she is a widow and proud parent of beautiful Nina Yvette.

Daisy L. Machado was ordained in 1981 as the first Latina ordained minister in the Christian Church (Disciples of Christ). She holds degrees from Brooklyn College (BA), College School of Social Work (MSW), Union Theological Seminary in New York City (MDiv), and the University of Chicago Divinity School (PhD). She is professor of church history at Union Theological Seminary. She served previously as academic dean, Lexington Theological Seminary, making her the first Latina dean of an Association of Theological Schools seminary in the United States. A native of Camagüey, Cuba, she immigrated with her parents to New York City at age three.

Loida I. Martell-Otero is associate professor of constructive theology at Palmer Theological Seminary, in Wynnewood, Pennsylvania. A bi-coastal Puerto Rican, she holds degrees from the University of Puerto Rico (BS), Tuskegee University School of Veterinary Medicine (DVM), Andover Newton Theological School (MDiv), and Fordham University (MPhi and PhD). An ordained American Baptist Churches/USA minister, she has fifteen years of pastoral experience. She has written on Latina *evangélica* theology and soteriology and coedited *Teología en Conjunto: A Collaborative Hispanic Protestant Theology* with José D. Rodríguez.

Denise R. Mason has served as pastor of Community of Reconciliation Church, Pittsburgh, Pennsylvania, since 2000. An ordained minister in the United Church of Christ, she has also served Peoples Congregational United

Church of Christ, Washington, D.C., and served on the national staff of the her denomination in Cleveland, Ohio. She is a graduate of Howard University School of Divinity and is the author of numerous articles on congregational revitalization and worship.

Carol Antablin Miles, an ordained minister in the Presbyterian Church (USA), holds degrees from the University of California at Berkeley (AB), the University of Southern California (MA), and Princeton Theological Seminary (MDiv and PhD). She currently serves as associate professor of preaching at Luther Seminary, St. Paul, Minnesota.

Minh-Hanh Nguyen was born in Saigon, Vietnam, and came to the United States in 1975. She had a long career in vocational rehabilitation for persons with disabilities prior to being ordained in the Evangelical Lutheran Church in America in 1999. A peace and justice activist, she served two Anglo ELCA congregations until January 2006, when she was called as associate rector of St. Anselm Episcopal Church, Garden Grove, California, under the full communion partnership signed between the denominations.

Zaida Maldonado Pérez, a native of Puerto Rico, is associate professor of theological studies at Asbury Theological Seminary (Dunnam campus, Florida). Prior to this, she was director of the Hispanic Theological Initiative. Zaida earned an MDiv from Eden Theological Seminary and a PhD from Saint Louis University. She is coauthor of *An Introduction to Christian Theology* and is a member of the United Church of Christ.

Gayll Phifer-Houseman served with InterVarsity Christian Fellowship for seventeen years at San Jose State University, University of California–Berkeley, and Stanford University. She received her master's degree in cross-cultural studies, leadership emphasis, from Fuller Theological Seminary. Currently she directs The Father's House, a retreat ministry of prayer and renewal. With her husband, Mark, and children Ephrem, Meheretab, Yodit, and Bethlehem, she actively participates in The River Church Community, a nondenominational church. Gayll is of Dutch/German descent and has embraced Ethiopia and Ethiopian culture through her children.

Debbie Royals, Pascua Yaqui, is an Episcopal priest. She serves as regional missioner for Native Ministry Development in the Dioceses of Los Angeles and Northern California and is the Indigenous People's Network Chair for Province VIII in the Episcopal Church. Debbie also teaches as a health professional faculty member of CREDO, a collaborative alliance that provides intensive opportunities for clergy and laypeople's vocational discernment.

Melva L. Sampson serves as the project manager for the Sisters Chapel WISDOM Center at Spelman College. She is a nonprofit program administration professional, creative writer, and ordained minister. Her published and presented works include "After Katrina and Rita: What Must I Do to Be Saved?" which appears in *The Sky Is Crying: Race, Class, and Natural Disaster,* and an American Academy of Religion presentation, "Give Me Body: The Black Female Body as Icon in Hip-Hop and Religious Culture." Her current research is titled "Dancing in the Spirit: Rhythmic Movement in Hip-Hop 'Krumping' Dance Culture as Liberative Praxis of Hope and Resistance." She holds degrees from Virginia Union University in Richmond, Virginia (BA, history and political science); Howard University (Patricia Roberts Harris Public Affairs Fellow, human communications studies, MA); and Candler School of Theology at Emory University (MDiv).

Gina M. Stewart, a native of Memphis, pastors the church in which she was reared, Christ Missionary Baptist Church, as the first African American woman elected to serve an established African American Baptist congregation in Memphis/Shelby County. She received degrees from the University of Memphis (BBA), Trevecca Nazarene College (ME, administration and supervision), Memphis Theological Seminary (MDiv), and The Interdenominational Theological Center (DMin). She has received numerous honors and awards. In addition, she serves or has served on several boards, including Big Brothers and Big Sisters and the Samuel DeWitt Proctor Pastors' Conference.

Lisa M. Tait, co-pastor of Imani Christian Center, Stone Mountain, Georgia, serves as founder and CEO of Women of Destiny Ministries (www.womenofdestiny.org), a nonprofit organization. She also serves as adjunct professor at the Interdenominational Theological Center. She authored *Women of Destiny: Five Principles for Pursuing Your Purpose in God.* She holds degrees from Howard University (BS), The American University (MA), and the Samuel DeWitt Proctor School of Theology at Virginia Union University (MDiv, DMin). She is married to the Rev. Dr. Lewis T. Tait Jr., with whom she parents children Essence Ayana and Lewis T. Asante Tait III.

Veronica Martin Thomas, a native of Monroe, Louisiana, lives in Norfolk, Virginia, with her husband, Winfred Thomas Sr. She is a member of Messiah

Presbyterian Church and a candidate for minister of Word and sacrament. She holds a MDiv degree from Union Theological Seminary and Presbyterian School of Christian Education in Richmond, Virginia.

Christine Y. Wiley pastors Covenant Baptist Church with her husband, Dennis, in Washington, D.C. They have three adult children and four grandchildren. She directs the theological field education department at the Howard University School of Divinity. She is a fellow of the American Association of Pastoral Counselors and has written numerous articles and chapters about the church, mental health, and depression.

Sakena D. Young-Scaggs, an ordained itinerant elder in the African Methodist Episcopal Church, holds degrees from Boston University (MDiv and MST). She served as Protestant chaplain at Brown University and associate dean of Marsh Chapel at Boston University. She currently is a doctoral candidate at Drew University in ethics and sociology of religion through its religion and society program. She now resides in Montclair, New Jersey, with her spouse, the Rev. Jonathan Young-Scaggs, and her children Ashé, Najé, Felicia, and Marcel.

Meet *These* Preaching Women!

(Book cover images, beginning top left, from left to right)

Row 1: Donna Allen, E. Anne Henning Byfield, Dionne Boissière, Valerie Bridgeman Davis, Gennifer Benjamin Brooks, Carla Jean-McNeil Jackson

Row 2: Elizabeth Conde-Frazier, Helen Bessent Byrd, Daisy L. Machado, Phyllis Thompson Hilliard, Anne-Marie Jeffery, Yvette Flunder

Row 3: Sakena D. Young-Scaggs, Emily C. Hassler, Holly Haile Davis, Lisa Wilson Davison, EunJoung Joo, Portia Wills Lee

Row 4: Liala Ritsema Beukema, MarQuita A. Carmichael Burton, Carol Antablin Miles, Denise R. Mason, Zaida Maldonado Pérez, Gina M. Stewart

Row 5: Loida I. Martell-Otero, Melva L. Sampson

Row 6: Gayll Phifer-Houseman, Lisa M. Tait

Row 7: Christine Y. Wiley, Veronica Martin Thomas

Row 8: Minh-Hanh Nguyen, Debbie Royals

Row 9: Wil Gafney